Beyond Flesh and Blood
The Ultimate Guide To Angels and Demons

Minister Dante Fortson

Beyond Flesh and Blood
The Ultimate Guide To Angels and Demons

Copyright © 2012 by Minister Dante Fortson

Website: www.ministerfortson.com

ISBN 10: 1466239816
ISBN 13: 978-1466239814

All scripture quotations in this book are taken from the King James Version of the Bible except where noted. Words appearing in bold are the author's own emphasis.

All rights reserved. No portion of this book may be reproduced or transmitted in any form or by any means, electronic or mechanical, including photocopying, recording, or by an information storage and retrieval system, without the written permission of the author.

First Edition. Printed in the United States of America

Editors: Taneka Dickson

Published by: Impact Agenda Media

TABLE OF CONTENTS

- ☐ Acknowledgments
- ☐ Introduction
- ☐ What Is Spiritual Warfare?

Angels 101: The Nature of Angels

- ☐ Chapter 1: Angelology and Demonology 101
- ☐ Chapter 2: What Are Angels?
- ☐ Chapter 3: The Ranks of Angels

Angels 102: A Supernatural Society

- ☐ Chapter 4: The Rise of An Adversary
- ☐ Chapter 5: The War In Heaven
- ☐ Chapter 6: The Abilities of Angels
- ☐ Chapter 7: The Origin of Demons

Angels 103: The History of Angels

- ☐ Chapter 8: The Technology of Angels
- ☐ Chapter 9: Supernatural Deception
- ☐ Chapter 10: The Destiny of Angels and Demons

Bonus Material and Resources

- ☐ About The Author
- ☐ Appendix A: Scenario X

Acknowledgements

First and foremost I want to thank my Lord and Savior Jesus (Yeshua) for allowing me to complete this, my fourth book. Next I want to thank my wife Jenelle and my mom Pastor Perryetta Lacy for listening to endless hours of new research, discoveries, and strange theories. I appreciate it. Finally I would like to thank the following people for all the love and support that I have received over the years: Brian Lacy, Derrius, Taneka Dickson, Stanford Greenlee, Kareem Muller, Sis. Mary, Sis. Norma, J Rich, Xavier Jackson, Kwon, Dori Lynn, King Wells, Keith Well, Doug Riggs, Connie Huft, Jim Wilhelmsen, Rob Roselli, Proof Negative, Steve Quayle, Chuck Missler, Grant Jeffrey, Marvin Bittinger, L.A. Marzulli, all of my Omega Hour guests, all of my readers, and the entire Ignited Praise Fellowship family. If I missed anyone by name, please believe it was not intentional. May God continue to bless and keep you all.

Foreword

Who is the devil? Does the devil command an army? What is the level of power the devil really has? Why do what we call fallen angels look like some of the creatures we see in ancient mythology? Who or what is the *nachash*? How is the spiritual war between Satan and God being fought on earth?

Beyond Flesh and Blood contains a great deal of new and important information about angels and the spirit realm in general. It shows how this war is reflected in every culture on earth and how every man must make a decision on whose side he/she is on.

Minister Dante Fortson breaks down the supernatural and biological warfare that Satan has been using against God and humanity. He illustrates how the fallen angels have technology, and how they have issued technology to influence humanity. He goes to show how the angels have a language all their own.

You will learn a great deal by reading this book; and hopefully, be motivated to dig deeper into the things of God and His Holy Bible. We are in the last of the last days. Time is very short and we must be prepared for the supernatural events that are soon to hit this world like a hurricane. Do not be caught unawares! This book will help you be prepared. Good work Dante!

King S Wells Jr.

Host, *TEOTWAWKII* Radio
Author of *Ancient Myths and The Bible*

Introduction

There have been many books written about the supernatural, but very few written by people that have experienced it from both sides of the issue. Although I have been a Christian since around the age of five or six, my initial journey into the spirit realm was not by choice. I remember having a toy Noah's Ark that I would play with in the bath tub, but only knew about the animals going in two by two. In hind sight it was almost prophetic. That toy was one of the first toys I actually remember having as a child, and later in life that story and every detail surrounding it would become my obsession. Over the course of my life I have encountered spirits both good and hostile. I have dabbled in astral projection, channeling, and a lot more. This is only part of the reason that I feel qualified to write a book of this nature.

Why I Wrote This Book

When I was growing up there was no one that I could talk to about the supernatural, so I snuck and read ghost stories even though my mom told me not to. I kept the doors to spiritual influence open without even knowing it. My goal is to provide a resource for people that may have gone through or may be going through some of the same things that I experienced. This book was written to let people know that they are not alone and that every supernatural occurrence in the history of mankind can be found in the 66 books we call the Bible.

We as Christians are sometimes not willing to take an honest look into things that we assume may not be true or we shrug it off by referring to it as "mythology". The spiritual realm is very real and because we are on the front lines, we need to understand our enemy. Those that believe we should not dabble in the supernatural are 100% correct, but gaining knowledge about one's enemy is not the same as dabbling. If we are not supposed to know anything about our enemy, why would the inspired word of God give us so much information about them? Many of the books written about spiritual warfare only talk about the armor of God and repeat some of the same things we have already learned. Beyond Flesh and Blood takes spiritual warfare to the next level by examining our enemy from a Biblical perspective and tying those conclusions into real world events and encounters reported throughout history. I believe that once we understand the nature of spiritual warfare, we will be better equipped to fight the battle. Before any army goes into battle, they do their very best to gather information on the enemy that they are dealing with. We as Christians should be no less equipped with knowledge than as if we were in an actual war; because we are. In fact our war is being fought on multiple levels, which means obtaining knowledge is mandatory for us to stay in this fight.

Hebrew, Greek, and Latin

Throughout this book I will refer back to the Hebrew, Greek, and Latin languages because sometimes the original meanings were much different than what church tradition and translation conveys at times. It is through studying the original languages that we begin to make sense of many things that appear in the Bible. One thing that many people fail to consider, including myself at times, is that the KJV has shaped most of our modern views on the Bible, but the Bible was not originally written in English. I will say up front that I prefer the KJV over any version out there, so most of the quotes in this book will come from that version. Something else that needs to be understood about these three languages is that they are very precise and often more descriptive than English. Sometimes it takes as much as a full sentence to properly translate a single word into English. We also know from experience that English words and meaning change very quickly. Words that mean one thing today may not mean the same thing tomorrow.

My Use of Outside Texts

Introduction

The spiritual realm was not only experienced by the Hebrews, but by every culture on earth, and were recorded in the stories we have come to refer to as "mythology". My use of texts outside of the Bible is not to prove the Bible by using them, but to compare and contrast similar events and beliefs. While the Hebrews focused mainly on God, pagan cultures kept detailed records of supernatural beings that they worshipped as the gods. Unfortunately, we have been taught that these ancient stories were nothing more than mythology, but that explanation does not seem to add up once we begin digging for the truth. As our culture progresses, many things that we believed to be mythology are slowly becoming reality. I believe that some of these texts offer significant insight into the spiritual realm.

I also believe that there is a behind the scenes struggle to hide the true nature of the spiritual realm from mankind. For example, when we look at different cultures we find very similar events, but names and places have been changed. We find concepts that that are very familiar, but referred to by different names. One such occurrence is Karma vs. "reaping what you sow". Karma comes from Hindu teachings and reaping what you sow comes from the Bible. However, a brief study of the two concepts reveals that they are almost the exact same concept under a different name. Throughout this book we will explore many more similarities like this. The above similarity is just one reason that I think it is important to understand other cultures and what they teach.

What Is The Bible?

I believe the Bible is the center piece in the cosmic puzzle. I think of it as sort of a CliffsNotes of human history. The Bible is the summary of events that point the way to the Messiah, Yeshua/Jesus. From Genesis to Revelation, the Bible focuses on the need for a redeemer, His coming, His sacrifice, and salvation through Him. The Bible is also the blueprint to the ultimate reality. It can be used to validate every kind of supernatural event that has ever been reported in the history of mankind. From vampires to alien abduction, the Bible hints at something going on in the spiritual realm that we are only getting a glimpse of here on earth. I believe we should be familiar with and aware of what other cultures teach, not as scripture, but as their perspective of supernatural events in history. If we ignore the names such as gods, djinn, shevas, etc., and break it down to an attribute comparison; we may find that the myths and legends from around the world are really about mischievous fallen angels posing as something other than what they really are.

The Bible provides the only foundation of truth in matters of the supernatural. Without it we run the risk of being swayed by every wind of doctrine. It is because of this that I use the Bible as the blueprint for my research. Instead of working to make the Bible fit my preconceived notions, I allow the Bible to guide the direction of my research.

My Opinions in This Book

Over the last few years I have come to realize that there are many books out there that express their opinion on what different parts of the Bible are really saying. Everything you find in this book is just my opinion at best, and you will likely not agree with everything that I write. We will not fully know if we are correct or incorrect until Christ returns, and I've heard Chuck Missler point out that some Jews believe that when the Messiah returns, He will interpret the words, the letters, and the spaces between the letters. Again, the ideas expressed in this book are just my opinion on the subject of spiritual realm, and my opinions are subject to change as new information becomes available. I am by no means "married" to any of the concepts in this book, except that Jesus (Yeshua) is the only way to salvation. I am also a firm believer that we should change our beliefs to fit the Bible, not change the Bible to fit our beliefs.

Where Do We Go From Here?

My hope is that you will check everything that I have written in this book. Acts 17:11 should be at the forefront of every Christian's mind when studying any text, no matter who it's written by or how long ago it was written. As you begin your study of spiritual warfare, you will encounter angelology, demonology, numerology, and several other "ologies". The most important thing to understand when undertaking a study like this is to pray without ceasing. May God bless you and keep you on your quest for spiritual growth.

Sincerely,

Minister Dante Fortson

Minister Dante Fortson

What Is Spiritual Warfare?

Spiritual warfare is a very important subject that, in my opinion, is not emphasized enough in the Christian community. While it may be discussed, it is usually in an abstract sense, as if it is as simple as being delayed to work, church, or health issue. While those examples may be the results of supernatural influence, spiritual warfare is much deeper than that. The following excerpts on spiritual warfare are from people that are very familiar with the subject.

Jim Wilhelmsen

Spiritual warfare is the description of a state of war that exists by a rebel alliance led by Satan against God and his creation. It is called spiritual warfare because of its origin but most people believe that it is restricted or limited to the spirit realm by spirit beings. What is not understood is that the entities involved are both physical as fallen angels of many different types, and physical characteristics and disembodied spirits called demons. They are both behind the scenes working their evil against God and man, but also in our midst in a physical form working on that level as well. The weapons given to us by the Lord are the Holy Spirit and God's Word in application by faith; and they are not restricted to the spiritual plane, they are fully effective on all levels to overcome the enemy. Jesus is Lord of all on any level, He is the same yesterday, today and forever.

C. A. Huff

From personal experience and Biblical sources we know that we struggle not against flesh and blood, but against UNSEEN forces. We feud and rival with forces beyond our comprehension, like a battle of the blind against an enemy who would seem to have an unfair advantage. But yet the bible tells us we have invisible armor to protect us; words that are stored in our heart, when enabled to come from our mouths have the ability to tear down strongholds, build empires in the spiritual realms, and put up fortified walls—firewalls of protection against this unseen enemy. We can turn the tides of torment from our tormentors onto themselves, choking them, and burning them with searing hot pokers of righteousness, and only with power that comes from the eternal almighty God.

Love, the most powerful of the weapons—is the one that is the most forgotten—and yet without this invisible weapon, we are told we are nothing but clanging gongs, even though we parade around as war generals and demand homage from our liege. No—love comes in the form of a humble servant, one who cares not of his position but wields its devastating power toward its abusers and sends them to a fiery abyss, while lavishing compassion, and healing and salvation on its former victims. Spiritual warfare veterans making in-roads in the trenches of hell are humble warriors, knowing what they themselves have been saved from, willing to risk ridicule, make mistakes, and wallow in the filth of the enemy in order to free a captive soul who yearns, but does not know a loving, and just God. It is sharing scarred memories, haunting times, and trying to find words and actions to express to others the salvation you yourself did not deserve. Praise to a Mighty God, Jesus Christ, who is key to my salvation, it's an honor to fight in the army of the Lord!

As the Body of Christ approaches her final translation or catching away (Greek *harpazo* 1 Thessalonians 4:17) we will face Satan's' final all-out assault in his vicious attempt to destroy his nemesis the Church (Matthew 16:18; 1 Corinthians 6:3; 1 Peter 4:7, 12-19; 5:8-11 etc.). It is extremely important for us to understand the background of Ephesians 6:10-17 as God's call for the Body of Christ put on the full armor of God in the context of the above cited scriptures. Of first importance the series of Aorist imperatives represent an urgent and immediate command given by the Holy Spirit through the Apostle Paul for all believers to "be strong" (vs. 10), "put on" (vs. 11), "take up" (vs.13). These commands are all in the plural and given to the Church universal and not intended in the first instance as something individual and isolated. The Old Testament background references Paul is citing are taken from Isaiah 11:5 and 59:16ff. The context for these passages cited is the second coming of Jesus Christ to this earth to deliver Israel, judge the Gentile nations, destroy the armies of anti-christ and inaugurate His 1,000 year millennial reign. These Old Testament prophecies reveal that the victorious Messiah returns clothed in the "full armor of God"! Before he returns the defeat the armies of anti-christ the Church, the Body of Christ corporately must first attain (Greek *katantao* = reach the goal) unto the mature manhood of Jesus Christ defined as "the measure of the stature of the fullness of Christ" (Ephesians 4:13), "put on the Lord Jesus Christ" in character and conduct (Romans 13:14). It is in this context that the Holy Spirit speaking through Paul exhorts the Church, the Body of Christ corporately to "take up the full armor of God, that you (plural 'you all') may be able to resist (hold your ground and not retreat) in the evil day (Greek the day-the evil), having done everything, to stand firm".

The adjective "evil" modifying the noun "day" both have the definite article which is striking and can be paraphrased 'the day that is particularly and specifically evil'. Was the Holy Spirit warning the Church His Apostle of a final end-time battle between Satan with his evil forces and the Body of Christ preceding and preparing the way for the revelation of the anti-christ? (2 Thessalonians 2:1-12) I firmly believe this is exactly what was in his mind when he wrote this circular epistle to the Church at Ephesus. Referring back to verse 10 of this chapter we can amplify and expand the rich meaning of the Greek text by translating this verse: 'Finally, to sum everything up, habitually allow yourselves to go on receiving power from within (Greek pres. pass. imptv. of endunamao = be empowered from within) in union with the Lord, and in the strength of His might'. Let us all take this passage seriously with this in mind so that our Lord Jesus Christ may receive, through a prepared remnant in these last days, all that he requires through His Church to see this age consummated! Remember, the Body of Christ corporately is defined as "one new man" with Christ as the Head the Church as His Body (Ephesians 2:15.). The Head and Body together are also defined as "the Christ" (1 Corinthians 12:12). When Jesus returns with his glorified Bride, the Church at the second advent, He returns to be glorified in His saints on that day....(2 Thessalonians 1:10). What a glorious calling!

> "Behold; I give unto you the power to tread on snakes and scorpions..." - Luke 10:19

One of the most important things I've learned about spiritual warfare which leads to victory over the demonic attacks that do come against you as a born again Christian is knowing who you are in Jesus Christ. That being a born again believer means being endowed with power from on high, and the right, through the shed blood of Jesus and faith in Him to command, and bind demons and rebuke their insidious attacks. When we ask these things, in Jesus name *they must obey*, as by His name *every knee shall bow*, you have the authority in Christ to ask Him to take these *things* to wherever he takes them until the time of their judgment. One of the weapons in my arsenal against these evil entities that they seem to particularly detest; is after binding them, you ask Jesus to assign one of His angels to sing hymns of worship and praise 24/7 until the time of their judgment. It almost seems to cause them to think twice before launching an attack. They hate songs of worship and praise. Just think about any movie, book or play you are familiar with and I can almost guarantee there is a celebration after an intense battle has been won! Singing the songs yourself is even better as it becomes a triumphant hymn of victory over darkness to sing with passion and joy; for greater is He that is within thee than he that is in the world!

Closing doors, and breaking generational curses back to the 5th or 6th generation will also assist you in keeping out the nasty intruders. Remember; Satan roams about, like a roaring lion seeking whom he may devour. Don't leave yourself vulnerable; confess your sins, repent, and renounce them every day as we are all sinners and fall short of the glory of God. Closing doors means examining your life with the help of the Holy Spirit and asking to be shown where you may be holding open a door to the demonic. Satan is a legalist, if he thinks he has a legal right to provoke you, you need to break that right by turning away from the activities that might give him a toe hold. This doesn't mean you won't get attacked for if you are truly praying against dark forces, binding them, rebuking them and casting them out in Jesus name; you are a warrior and are going to do battle; it goes with the territory.

Angels 101: The Nature of Angels

Chapter 1: Angelology and Demonology 101

> "I was bold in the pursuit of knowledge, never fearing to follow truth and reason to whatever results they led, and bearding every authority which stood in their way." - Thomas Jefferson

Angelology and demonology seem to be two highly controversial and mostly avoided subjects in the modern Church. Part of the reason seems to be fear of the subject and the other part seems to be lack of education on the subject. When beginning a study of this nature, it is inevitable that certain objections will be encountered. Some of these objections are valid and some of them are nothing more than opinions without merit or Biblical backing. Before beginning a study of this nature, there are three things we need to keep in mind:

- Pray
- Pray
- Pray

Taking up a study in angelology or demonology is taking a step beyond the normal everyday Sunday School version of spiritual warfare that we encounter in our daily lives. This is why the Bible tells us to pray without ceasing (1 Thessalonians 5:17). In this chapter we are going to address some of the objections and obstacles we should expect to encounter while undertaking this study.

We Don't Need To Know These Things

This is possibly the most used objection against studying these "ologies", but is it justified or backed by the Bible? The Bible spends a great deal of time addressing the supernatural and specifically the subject of spiritual warfare. While a study of this nature is definitely not recommended for new Christians, it is both recommended and encouraged for those Christians that are ready to move from milk to meat.

> "When I was a child, I spake as a child, I understood as a child, I thought as a child: but when I became a man, I put away childish things." - 1 Corinthians 13:11

There are many Christians that sit in the church and remain stagnant in their development because the pastor only teaches about salvation, faith, and similar issues. While there is nothing wrong with teaching those things, all real believers in Christ have already come to salvation through faith in Christ. Those are the very first steps to becoming a true Christian, and eventually we need to move past those things and educate ourselves on the rest of what God's word says. With that said, there are some exceptions to the rule of new Christians not being involved in a study of this nature. The exceptions would be people who are involved in the occult, communicating with spirits, practicing witchcraft, enduring night terrors/visitations, believe they are experiencing alien abduction, and many other things that have plunged them right into the middle of spiritual warfare. These people are far beyond Spiritual Warfare 101, and need to be made fully aware of what they are involved in.

This Takes The Focus Away From Christ

This is a completely false statement, but it is used all too often. In fact, an in depth study in spiritual warfare actually addresses the need and urgency of accepting Christ into one's life. As mentioned above, there are people already involved in spiritual warfare and they have no clue as to what is really going on. Unfortunately, if the Church does not make the body of Christ aware of what is going on in the world, many of the people in need of Christ will be lost to the deception that they are currently enduring.

We Should Ignore These Things

Ignoring the problem does not make it go away. In fact, it usually makes the problem worse. We can look at the current focus of our society as proof of that. Almost any night of the week, we can turn on the TV and find a show featuring one or all of the following:

- Communicating With Spirits

Chapter 1: Angelology and Demonology 101

- Vampires
- Werewolves
- Ghosts
- UFOs and Aliens

The problem is that it is not Christians addressing these subjects, but worldly writers and producers putting their spin on spiritual matters. Because the Church does not address these issues, the only place to turn is to the secular media for an explanation. One byproduct of this large scale avoidance of these subjects is an expansion of the Intelligent Design movement. At first it sounds like that might be a positive advance in favor of Christianity and belief in God, but that is not necessarily the case. The evidence of Intelligent Design is too overwhelming to ignore and evolution is no longer holding the weight it previously did. Instead of professing a belief in God, people are ascribing the obvious design in nature to Ancient Aliens. The History Channel has made this theory very popular with three seasons and two documentaries that are based around the Ancient Astronaut Theory. One reason that it is referred to as the Ancient Astronaut theory is because it is not just about aliens. Some of the theories propose that the source of many modern technologies and UFO sightings are survivors of Atlantis, humans from the future, and aliens from other planets. This theory has the potential to be much bigger than evolution because the evidence of something else out there is overwhelming:

> "For the mystery of iniquity doth already work: only he who now letteth will let, until he be taken out of the way. And then shall that Wicked be revealed, whom the Lord shall consume with the spirit of his mouth, and shall destroy with the brightness of his coming: Even him, whose coming is after the working of Satan with all power and signs and lying wonders, And with all deceivableness of unrighteousness in them that perish; because they received not the love of the truth, that they might be saved. And for this cause God shall send them strong delusion, that they should believe a lie: That they all might be damned who believed not the truth, but had pleasure in unrighteousness." - 2 Thessalonians 2:7-1

The New Age teaching regarding the above is that Satan is really part of an advanced alien race and will eventually return to earth. They are also expecting a Christ-like figure that will be an alien/human hybrid. We as Christians refer to this Christ-like figure as Antichrist. They even have their own version of the Rapture that explains away the disappearance of humans as an alien cleansing of archaic beliefs. This is just one of many reasons that the Church should not be ignoring the subject of spiritual warfare.

This Can Shake Someones Faith

This is a very justified objection and for those that are not ready, it is possible that a study like this could potentially shake their faith. For those that come out on the other side of a study like this, their faith will be much stronger than it has ever been before.

> "My brethren, count it all joy when ye fall into divers temptations; Knowing this, that the trying of your faith worketh patience. But let patience have her perfect work, that ye may be perfect and entire, wanting nothing. If any of you lack wisdom, let him ask of God, that giveth to all men liberally, and upbraideth not; and it shall be given him. But let him ask in faith, nothing wavering. For he that wavereth is like a wave of the sea driven with the wind and tossed." - James 1:2-6

One of the reasons that we pray during a study like this is because it is very draining both spiritually and physically. We will encounter things that sincerely cause us to question much of what we currently believe and it will definitely make us question many of the Church traditions we have been taught. Rest assured in the fact the James 1:2-6 confirms that this testing of our faith will benefit us in the end.

This Can Open Doorways

An in depth study in spiritual warfare can indeed open spiritual doorways, but that is why we need to continue to pray. Once a spiritual doorway has been opened, it can be difficult,

Chapter 1: Angelology and Demonology 101

but not impossible to close. Some activities that seem innocent can lead to very dangerous spiritual obsessions without us even noticing. These interests develop slowly and draw us in little by little. It may start with something as simple and seemingly innocent as reading the daily Horoscope, then progress into Tarot Cards, Psychic Readings, and before we know it we are into Astral Projection and contacting Spirit Guides. It does not always happen in that order or with those specific examples, but it does happen almost always without fail.

Before undertaking this study it is important to do a self assessment to determine if you currently have any spiritual doorways that are open. If you do, it is important to pray to have them closed before proceeding. Failing to close these doors before studying such a volatile subject as this can actually make things worse and not better. Here is a short list of the most common doorways that have usually been opened. This list is by no means complete, but it is a good place to start.

- Daily Horoscope Reading
- Consulting Psychics
- Tarot Card Readings
- Night Terrors
- Feeling of Strange Presences

As we progress through the book we will encounter many more possible doorways to demonic activity. If you recognize any of the doorways encountered in this book, and you believe they are open in your life, you should pray to have them closed immediately.

Withdrawal From Things Of God

In addition to shaken faith and spiritual doorways being constantly opened and closed, you may feel yourself begin to withdraw from church, the Bible, and even Christian friends. You may experience thoughts that conflict with what you believe or even experience a different voice in your head. This is when you need to take a break and do some heavy praying. From this point on when you begin to experience these thoughts, spiritual warfare will become more real and more intense than it has ever been.

Your World View Will Change

Once you begin to see how much of our world is spiritually influenced, your view of the world will likely change. You will begin to realize that it is no longer about black, white, red, blue, Democrat, or Republican. It simply comes down to good vs. evil and God vs. Satan.

> "For we wrestle not against flesh and blood, but against principalities, against powers, against the rulers of the darkness of this world, against spiritual wickedness in high places." - Ephesians 6:12

Soon you will begin to understand that the politics, scientific pursuits, and even religious trends of this world are not only influenced by people, but also by "spiritual wickedness in high places."

Why This Book is Relevant

Many people wonder why a book like this is even relevant at all, and that is a good question. The average Christian is not exposed to some of the concepts that will be presented in this book. There is usually no emphasis on the concept of actual spiritual warfare in the modern church and many of the supernatural events in the Bible are watered down in the pulpit. This book is relevant because it deals with end time spiritual warfare and if the pattern of scripture holds true, we can use past events to determine how future events may play out.

- **Genesis 6:** Fallen angels descend upon mankind and the ultimate result is God wiping out the world with a flood.
- **Genesis 19:** Two angels enter Sodom and the end result is Sodom and three other cities are wiped out by God's judgment.
- **Exodus 12:** The angel of death kills the first born in Egypt as judgment for not releasing God's people.

Chapter 1: Angelology and Demonology 101

- **2 Samuel 24**: The angel of the Lord is sent to the threshing floor to hand out judgment.
- **2 Kings 19**: The angel of the Lord kills 185,000 Assyrians.
- **Revelation**: Angels hand out judgment upon all of mankind in the last days.

The Bible is clear that angels are the death dealers of heaven that administer God's judgment upon mankind. They are not simply invisible spirits or chubby winged babies that whisper ideas in people's ear. Angels are powerful, immortal, supernatural beings that have the free will to do good or evil, and we as Christians need to fully understand what that means in relation to spiritual warfare. The Bible is clear that our fight is not with flesh and blood, but with powerful, deceptive, supernatural beings that want nothing less than to overthrow God and damn all mankind to the Lake of Fire. Those that do not acknowledge that there is a real war going on for the souls of men will become casualties in a war that goes beyond flesh and blood.

Beyond Flesh and Blood

Many times we hear the term spiritual warfare but fail to grasp just how serious it is. Many people in important positions of power do not worship the God of the Bible. In fact, some of them openly deny God and the power of Christ. The ranks of government and the military are filled with people that are members of secret societies that have secret rituals and doctrines. These very same people make decisions that are passed down and affect the lives of those of us lower on the social ladder.

One such example is the current scientific pursuits of transhumanism and hybridization. These are based on the lies of Satan in the Garden of Eden, "ye shall be like gods". Hitler embraced a belief in transhumanism and the idea that he could create a master race of god-men through the process of eugenics. Hybridization has become a very popular subject on TV and in movies such as Splice and many others. This war on all flesh does indeed extend beyond the bounds of mortal men and threatens to affect the very nature of what it means to be human.

The Breakdown

Before beginning this study, you need to be 100% sure that you are ready for such an undertaking. This book is not intended to recruit you into spiritual warfare, but to enlighten you about the war that is already raging around you, whether you know it or not.

> "This is your last chance. After this there is no turning back. You take the blue pill, the story ends, you wake up in your bed and believe whatever you want to believe. You take the red pill, you stay in wonderland and I show you how deep the rabbit hole goes. Remember, all I'm offering is the truth, nothing more." – Morpheus, The Matrix

Chapter in Review

- Do we need to know about spiritual warfare?
- Does spiritual warfare take the focus off of Christ?
- Should we ignore spiritual warfare?
- Can this study shake someone's faith?
- Can this study open spiritual doorways?
- Can this study make someone withdraw from the things of God?
- Can this study change someone's world view?
- Why is this book relevant?
- Does spiritual warfare go beyond flesh and blood?

Critical Thinking

- Is spiritual warfare something I need to be concerned with?
- Am I ready for a study like this?
- What are the consequences of doing this study?

The Plan of Salvation

The plan of salvation is not difficult or complicated at all. In fact it can be summed up in one single verse. All you need to do in order to be saved is the following:

> That if thou shalt confess with thy mouth the Lord Jesus, and shalt believe in thine heart that God hath raised him from the dead, thou shalt be saved." – Romans 10:9

If you have accepted Christ, your next step should be to get your hands on a King James Version of the Bible. Before joining any church, you should have a good foundation in scripture without the influences of any teacher. Once you have a general understanding of scripture, visit a few churches before deciding on a church home. Make sure you check behind the pastor and do not just accept their word for anything without checking (Acts 17:11). If asking questions is discouraged, steer clear of that church at all costs.

Key Scriptures For Review

- 1 Corinthians 13
- 2 Thessalonians 2
- James 1
- Ephesians 6

Submit Your Questions

If you have more questions about spiritual warfare, angels, demons, the supernatural, or the Bible in general, you are welcome to submit your questions to me personally. Answers to your questions will be posted as an article on the website for everyone to see.

www.MinisterFortson.com

Chapter 2: What Are Angels?

> "Pride is still aiming at the best houses: Men would be angels, angels would be gods. Aspiring to be gods, if angels fell; aspiring to be angels men rebel." - Alexander Pope

Much of what we know about angels is based more on Church tradition than what the Bible actually says about them. There are many different beliefs as to when angels were created and for what purpose they were created. The Bible actually gives us many clues as to when the angels where created, and in addition to this, there are texts from other cultures that seem to support what the Bible says concerning angels. In this chapter we are going to discover when angels were created and possibly why angels were created.

When Were Angels Created?

There are many people that believe angels were created during the seven days described in the book of Genesis, but there are others that believe angels were created prior to the events in Genesis 1, but which group has it right? This question is possibly one of the easiest to find in the scripture and is also supported by many stories from other cultures.

> "Where wast thou when I laid the foundations of the earth? declare, if thou hast understanding. Who hath laid the measures thereof, if thou knowest? or who hath stretched the line upon it? Whereupon are the foundations thereof fastened? or who laid the corner stone thereof; When the morning stars sang together, and all the sons of God shouted for joy?" - Job 38:4-7

These verses lead many to believe that angels witnessed the creation of the earth, which means that they had to have been created prior to the creation of the earth. If this is indeed the case, which it seems to be, angels have been around for a very long time. In fact, before time was time. This also raises several more questions that we will need to eventually answer:

- Why were angels created in the first place?
- If angels are only messengers as is commonly believed, what did they do before the creation of people?

- If angels were only created to worship God, when did Lucifer have time to raise a rebellion?

As we continue we will attempt to answer these questions and many more. While taking up a study in angelology, it is impossible to ignore the gods of mythology, which have many characteristics in common with the angels of the Bible, including the timeframe in which they were created. Some of the other common themes shared between the angels and the gods are:

- Created by a higher power.
- One main god/angel that chooses to rebel.
- A war takes place in heaven.
- The rebels begin to lust after human women.
- Legendary hybrid offspring are born.

This will become extremely important later when we attempt to make sense of the many pagan beliefs surrounding the "gods" and their interaction with humankind. For now, let's focus on several beliefs from the Bible and other surrounding cultures as to the possible timeframe of angelic creation. Again, this is just one view, but it seems to fill in the blanks of the angelic timeline. If the angels did indeed have some kind of civilization, it would explain why they seem to have military ranks, rules, assignments, and access to strange technologies that defied human capability at the time.

Where Do Angels Fit Into History?

Hesiod was a Greek historian that believed that there was another race of human like beings that lived in paradise and never aged. They died when they were very old, but at death they were transformed into spirits that now interact with mankind. He referred to them as the Golden Race. Interestingly, there is a very controversial subject in the Bible that may indeed support Hesiod's belief. This belief is referred to as The Gap Theory. It is believed by many Christian scholars that it was during this gap in time that Satan planned his rebellion against God and was cast out of heaven.

Chapter 2: What Are Angels?

Our society is obsessed with angels, and nowhere is it more prevalent than in the New Age movement. Everywhere we turn, we can find something pertaining to angels. Images of chubby babies, glowing beings with halos, and wings fill our heads when we think of angels, but do angels really look like these depictions and what are they really? The existence of supernatural beings that are higher than humans, but lower than God is echoed throughout almost every culture on earth.

What Are Angels?

When asked the question, "what are angels?" the overwhelming response seems to be, "angels are messengers". In order to really understand what an angel is, we first need to toss out our preconceived notion of the word "angel". The word angel as we know it, is more of a job description than an actual definition of what the being is. By understanding the Greek and Hebrew words that refer to these entities, we can gain a better understanding of who we are fighting against and who we have on our side. The first word we need to address is the Greek word *aggelos*. The Greek word *aggelos* (*angelos*) means "messenger" or "bringer of tidings". This word can refer to a pastor or to the supernatural beings we refer to as angels. By definition, it does not describe what something is, but more correctly what their function or purpose is. While it is a great description of what they do, it does not answer the question of what angels are. For example, a pigeon, dog, or person can all serve as messengers, but that is not what they are. The answer to this question is very complicated to say the least, but the Bible does address this issue. There are those that say angels are simply spirits and therefore cannot physically interact with humans. There are others that say that angels are physical and can interact with humans freely. Thankfully, the Bible gives us the answer to this question.

In Genesis Chapter 18 Abraham sees three men approaching him and when they arrive he asks them to stay and eat with him. Later we find out that two of these men are actually angels on a mission from God to destroy the cities on the plain. If these were merely spiritual beings, how did they eat with Abraham? In Genesis Chapter 19 we find that the men of Sodom wanted to rape the same two angels that came to warn Lot of the pending destruction. In the beginning of the chapter, the Bible says that Lot saw two "men" approaching the city and he ran out to greet them. Lot was probably aware that these were not ordinary men because he seemed to be waiting for them, based on the context of the story. The men of Sodom were clearly convinced that they were ordinary men, which implies that angels look almost indistinguishable from humans. When the men in the city became a threat, the two angels grabbed Lot and pulled him back into the house to keep him safe. If these were purely spiritual beings, no one would have mistaken them for men and they would not have been able to pull Lot back into the house. There are many verses that describe angels physically interacting with mankind, but the Bible is clear that they are also spiritual beings (Psalm 104:4). However, there are several more verse that refer to angels as men and women.

Human Or Something Similar?

Are angels human or just something similar to human? The use of the words men and women to describe these beings is indeed one of the great mysteries that we encounter in the Bible. The following is a list of the angels referred to as men and women in the Bible.

- Satan (man – Isaiah 14:16)
- Gabriel (man – Daniel 9:21)
- Abraham's Visitors (men – Genesis 18:2)
- Lot's Visitors (men – Genesis 19:5)
- Angel of The Lord (man – Joshua 5:13)
- Angel That Wrestled Jacob (man – Genesis 32:24)
- Beings With The Ephah (women – Zechariah 5:9)

These references are very important in our understanding of what angels are. In the book of Isaiah we see whom many people believe to be Satan, being referred to as a man.

> "They that see thee shall narrowly look upon thee, and consider thee, saying, Is this the man that made the earth to tremble, that did shake kingdoms..." - Isaiah 14:16

Chapter 2: What Are Angels?

This is the chapter that contains the famous "Five I Wills" of Satan, but at this point, God is having Isaiah prophesy his destruction. During the prophecy, he refers to Satan as a man. Before we continue, let's look at another verse.

> "Yea, whiles I was speaking in prayer, even the man Gabriel, whom I had seen in the vision at the beginning, being caused to fly swiftly, touched me about the time of the evening oblation." - Daniel 9:21

It is interesting that two different prophets would refer to two different angels as men. Were they mistaking these angels for men or is there something far deeper going on that we do not yet understand? Let's look at one more reference by a third prophet before drawing any conclusions.

> "Then lifted I up mine eyes, and looked, and, behold, there came out two women, and the wind was in their wings; for they had wings like the wings of a stork: and they lifted up the ephah between the earth and the heaven." - Zechariah 5:9

Many believe this be a reference to female angels and it is possibly the only explanation as to why the pagan stories contain so many references to "goddesses", but the Bible has very little to say on the subject. If angels are different than humans, why do they choose to take on a human appearance? There are only two possible answers to that question:

- They take on a form that is easy for us to comprehend.
- They really look like men and women.

> "Be not forgetful to entertain strangers: for thereby some have entertained angels unawares." - Hebrews 13:2

Angels might actually be a creation very similar to humans, which would explain why we could have "entertained" them unaware. The closest we will probably get to understanding angels is what happed to Christ after the resurrection.

> "Beloved, now are we the sons of God, and it doth not yet appear what we shall be: but we know that, when he shall

> appear, we shall be like him; for we shall see him as he is." - John 1:32

John states that we are now the "sons of God" and we will be like Christ. After the resurrection, Christ displayed some very unique attributes previously only displayed in human interaction with angels. He could appear and disappear at will and walk through walls, but He could also be touched like He was still a living human.

> "Behold my hands and my feet, that it is I myself: handle me, and see; for a spirit hath not flesh and bones, as ye see me have." - Luke 24:39

Thank God for those people like Thomas that doubt, because without someone questioning this event in the Bible, we might not have had this insight. Some of the disciples believed Jesus might have been a spirit because He appeared out of nowhere (Luke 24:37), but as He pointed out, He is flesh and bone. Jesus clearly had a physical body, but He was capable of functioning as if He had no body at all. John stated that we will become like Him because "we are now sons of God". Jesus is the Son of God and He seemed to share the same abilities as the angels who are also referred to as sons of God (Genesis 6:4). Romans 8 is entirely about people becoming the sons of God, and Paul even points out the following:

> "For the earnest expectation of the creature waiteth for the manifestation of the sons of God." - Romans 8:19

In order to really understand what that verse is talking about, we first need to break down some of the components of this verse. The phrase "earnest expectation" is *apokardokia* in Greek, which means "eager expectation". The Greek word for "manifestation" is *apokalupsis*. You may recognize this word as the book titled "Revelation", which is the revealing of something. What this verse alludes to is that in our current form, we are not yet fully what we are intended to be, and because of that, all of creation is eagerly waiting for our full potential to be revealed.

Chapter 2: What Are Angels?

It seems that we become "more real" once we are changed and are able to interact with the physical and spiritual realms simultaneously. The best way to explain this would be to use The Matrix as an example. While in The Matrix, Neo could interact with people in any manner he wanted. He could eat, drink, fight, fly, stop bullets, have sex, and produce offspring. Neo could freely move between his world and the computer world, but the majority of the population had no idea what was going on. If the movie had time to explore the human reaction to what Neo could do, we would have seen that some people might have mistaken him for an angel, a god, or an alien, depending on what they chose to believe. Likewise, we are trying to explain beings that come from a portion of reality that is closed to us at the moment. All we can do is try to understand what they are, but a full realization will not be possible until we are changed into similar beings. It is also possible that angels were created in the exact state that they are in now. We cannot say for sure if they were something else in the past, but what we do know is that they are indeed spiritual beings capable of physical interaction and vice versa.

In the Bible, angels do not appear with wings stretched out and a glowing halo floating over their head. They are very discreet and usually unrecognizable as anything other than humans, except to certain people. As we can see, something about the physiology of angels when they are on earth resembles humans; however we do not know if angels have DNA or not when they take on a physical form. If they do, is it close enough to our own to enable reproduction? We also know from the scriptures that angels are made of celestial flesh and humans have terrestrial flesh. The question we now need to answer is, "are angels merely dead people with glorified bodies?"

Do Dead People Become Angels?

This is a question that many people have because it is often taught by some churches and completely ignored by others. Because of this, the issue is usually not addressed and people believe that angels are the spirits of the dead. While the Bible is unclear about exactly what angels are, here is what we learn in the Old Testament:

> "For thou hast made him a little lower than the angels, and hast crowned him with glory and honour." - Psalm 8:5

According to the Old Testament, while still in the flesh, people are just a little lower than the angels. The reason we know that this is true is because of a reference that the writer of Hebrews makes about Jesus.

> "But we see Jesus, who was made a little lower than the angels for the suffering of death, crowned with glory and honour; that he by the grace of God should taste death for every man." - Hebrews 2:9

We know that in the spirit, Jesus is much higher than the angels, but we see in the above verse that He was made lower than the angels for the purpose of dying. We know that this is a reference to Him becoming a physical man because of Psalm 8:5. Humans are the only beings mentioned in the Bible as being crowned with honor and glory. Even though this is not much to go on, we can conclude that angels, and humans that are still in the flesh, are not one and the same, but what about after people die?

> "Know ye not that we shall judge angels? how much more things that pertain to this life?" - 1 Corinthians 6:3

According to Paul, humans will judge angels, but there is no mention in the Bible of people judging each other, angels judging humans, or angels judging angels. By default, this implies that humans and angels are not the same thing. Dead people do not become angels and watch over the living. To further explain how we can be sure that this is true, let's look at what it means to be made in the image of God.

In The Image of God

Before we dive into the meat of this subject it is important to understand that Adam was made in God's image and every man after Adam was made in the image of their human father. Scripture testifies to this.

Chapter 2: What Are Angels?

> "And Adam lived an hundred and thirty years, and begat a son in his own likeness, and after his image; and called his name Seth:" – Genesis 5:3

As we see from scripture, Seth was born in the image of Adam, who was made in the image of God. All humans today are copies of copies of copies of copies. If you have ever dealt with images, then you know that copies of copies degrade with each copy until it is only a glimpse of what the original looked like. This is where we encounter an interesting chain of events. Adam was created perfect and without sin, but over time mankind became more and more sinful, and possibly lost any resemblance that they had to the original man (Adam). We do not find any physical description of Adam in the Bible, but we have an idea of what he looked like physiologically and what he could do in his perfected form. Jesus, Adam, and the angels are the only three that are referred to as "sons of God" before the resurrection of Christ. We know that Christ and the angels had similar supernatural abilities based on what the Bible says. The comparison chart below shows the supernatural similarities of Post Resurrection Christ to the angels:

Ability	Christ	Angels
Suddenly Appear	Luke 24	Acts 12
Physical Touch	Luke 24	Genesis 19
Eat Food	Matthew 26	Psalm 78
Ascend In The Air	Acts 1	Judges 13

If we are only looking at spiritual similarities, one could come to the conclusion that people become angels when they die. However, the Bible actually clarifies this for us in no less than three places.

> "For verily he took not on him the nature of angels; but he took on him the seed of Abraham." – Hebrews 2:16

The writer of Hebrews is 100% clear that Jesus did not take on the nature of the angels when Christ incarnated as a mortal man. This verse indicates that angels and people have completely different natures. Paul refers to Christ as the "last Adam", which gives us a little more insight into the situation.

> "And so it is written, The first man Adam was made a living soul; the last Adam was made a quickening spirit." - 1 Corinthians 15:45

Without the benefit of a Strong's Concordance, the significance of this verse is usually lost. According to Paul, Adam was made *zao psuche* (living soul) and Jesus was made *zoopoieo pneuma* (life giving spirit). Before we continue, it is important to understand that there are two different words translated as "made" in this verse:

- *Ginomai* - To come into being, to be transitioned from one realm/condition to another (Adam).
- *Eis* - Moved into a particular purpose or result (Jesus).

Both Adam and Jesus were the first of their kind. Adam was given life and Christ is the giver of life according to 1 Corinthians 15. There is no Biblical record of the angels being referred to as "living souls" or "life giving spirits". Humans and angels seem to be completely different beings with completely different purposes and destinies. While we are on the subject of spirits, let's look at what the Bible has to say about the many different types of spirits found in its pages.

Spirits According To The Bible

The subject of the differing kinds of spirits is rarely discussed in depth, and as a result, people have a tendency to just make up different kinds of spirits to explain different things. According to scripture there are at the very minimum fifteen different types of spirits:

Spirit of God (Genesis 1:2) - In the opening verses of Genesis we see the Spirit of God moving over the face of the water. Many people believe that this is who we refer to as the Holy Spirit.

Living Spirits (1 Corinthians 15:45) - During the six days of creation, God breathed a spirit into the being which He formed. This being came to be called mankind.

Chapter 2: What Are Angels?

Life Giving Spirit (1 Corinthians 15:45) - Besides God, this is the only spirit to be referred to as a life giving spirit. We know Him as Jesus/Yeshua.

Ministering Spirits (Hebrews1:14) - Angels, demons, and humans can all fall into this category. Ministering spirits testify to human beings that Christ is the Son of God. We see angels and the prophets doing this all throughout scripture, but the demons do this as well (Matthew 8:29 and Acts 16:17).

> "The same followed Paul and us, and cried, saying, These men are the servants of the most high God, which shew unto us the way of salvation." - Acts 16:17

Animal Spirits (Ecclesiastes 3:21) - This is the first and only place in the Bible that speaks of animals having a spirit.

Evil Spirits (Luke 7:21) - This description is usually a reference to demons. We will cover this type of spirit more in depth later.

Fire Spirits (Psalm 104:4) - This is the first time in the Bible that angels are referred to as fire/flaming spirits. There are two very similar beliefs in fire spirits from other cultures. The Cherokee worshiped the creator Yahowah as the Elder Fires. They believe that he is three, yet they worship him as one. In Islamic belief, the Djinn are considered to be spirits of smokeless fire similar to evil angels in the Bible.

Familiar Spirits (Leviticus 19:31) - These are the spirits that are consulted by witches and psychics.

Spirits of The Heavens (Zechariah 6:5) - These are the chariots (red, black, white, pale green) that Zechariah sees during his vision.

Unclean Spirits (Matthew 10:1) - This term is usually used in reference to demons. We will look at this phrase more in depth later.

Seducing Spirits (1 Timothy 4:1) - These are the kind of spirits that are prophesied to mislead people not strongly grounded in their faith during the end of the age.

Lying Spirits (1 Kings 22:22) - This type of spirit is mentioned when God asks for volunteers to mislead the false prophets.

Father of Spirits (Hebrews 12:9) – The reason that God is referred to as the Father of Spirits is pretty self explanatory.

Imprisoned Spirits (1 Peter 3:19) – Many researchers believe that this is a reference to the angels that sinned in Genesis 6. While the Bible does not contain details to this event, they are described in depth in the book of Enoch.

Female Spirits (Zechariah 5:9) – This is one of two places that mention female supernatural beings. The second one is highly controversial, and will be addressed later.

> "Let the LORD, the God of the spirits of all flesh, set a man over the congregation, Which may go out before them, and which may go in before them, and which may lead them out, and which may bring them in; that the congregation of the LORD be not as sheep which have no shepherd." – Numbers 27:16-17

It's important to note that no spirit is bound to doing just one job. Much like people who can serve multiple functions, the spirit world seems to be very similar. There is also the possibility that the spirit realm is not limited to just angels and demons.

Female Spirits In The Bible

Many researchers in this field, including myself, agree that the gods of mythology are what we Christians refer to as fallen angels, but that leaves the question, who or what were the goddesses? This question is a stumbling stone for many people because there are clearly female supernatural entities mentioned in other cultures, but angels are always described as appearing as men in the Bible, but there are actually two scriptures that make reference to female supernatural entities:

> "Then lifted I up mine eyes, and looked, and, behold, there came out two women, and the wind was in their wings; for they had wings like the wings of a stork: and they lifted up the ephah between the earth and the heaven." – Zechariah 5:9

Chapter 2: What Are Angels?

The context of the verse tells us that these were not regular women because they have wings. Even stranger is the fact that Zechariah does not bother to ask what they are. Because these women are not explained, there is a lot of speculation as to what they are. There are some that believe they are angels, some that believe they are spirits, and some that believe they are nothing more than a vision and there are no female spirits. When we encounter a situation similar to the one mentioned, all we can do is attempt to research it through the lens of oral Jewish tradition and other cultures that were focused on the gods and goddesses that they worshiped. There are several Jewish texts in which we find that their tradition did indeed reflect a belief in female angels:

- Midbar Kedemot
- Yalkut Hadash
- Talmud

With that said, we have to keep in mind that many of these non Jewish cultures did not have the spiritual benefit of Biblical discernment concerning these matters. In Greek mythology, we find a goddess that matches the Biblical description of the women in Zechariah 5. This goddess was known to the Greeks as Nike, the goddess of victory.

Carving of The Greek Goddess Nike

This goddess also seems to be the target in Christ's message to the church of Ephesus. The carving above was found in the city of Ephesus and it is of the goddess Nike. According to the Greeks, Nike would reward the victors of competition with a wreath as a crown. In contrast, Christ promises to reward those that *nikao* (overcome, victory) with fruit from the tree of life. The Greek word *nikao* comes from the word *nike* and there are also several other words that come from the word *nike*.

- Nicholas
- Nicola
- Nick
- Nikolai
- Nicolae
- Nils
- Klaas
- Nicole
- Ike
- Niki
- Nikita
- Nika
- Niketas
- Nico

In the letter to the Ephesians we find the first mention in the Bible to an obscure group of people referred to as the Nicolaitanes. The word Nicolaitanes is a compound word consisting of two Greek words that mean "to conquer the people", which leads some researchers to believe that the Nicolaitanes were conquering the people in a spiritual sense. There are others that believe the word is a reference to followers of Nicolaus who was considered by the Church to be a heretic.

Theory: The reference to the Nicolaitanes may be a reference to those that followed the goddess Nike. The actual meaning of the term is unclear, but based on Ephesus being the center of Nike worship, it seems just as plausible as the two more popular theories.

Jesus addressing a supernatural entity in His letter to the churches would not be out of the ordinary in the Bible. This same theme of addressing a spiritual entity or power behind the human authority is found in Isaiah 14 and Ezekiel 28. While it is plausible that Nike is being alluded to in the letter to the Ephesians, she is not the only female spirit that is referenced in the Bible.

The Origin of The Succubus Legend

The Succubus legend was very popular during medieval times, and according to legend, the Succubus was a female demon that would sexually seduce men while they were sleeping. Even though this belief gained popularity during medieval times, the legend of a sexual, female, supernatural entity goes back even further.

> "The wild beasts of the desert shall also meet with the wild beasts of the island, and the satyr shall cry to his fellow; the screech owl also shall rest there, and find for herself a place of rest." – Isaiah 34:14

In the King James Version of the Bible, the reference to a screech owl seems like no big deal. However, there are many people that have rightfully pointed out that something is strange about translating it as such.

- *Liyliyth* (Hebrew) – translated as "screech owl", but from the root word *layil* which means, "night specter."

Simply put, a specter is a ghost or apparition. Isaiah 34:14 clearly refers to liyliyth as a "her", which means we are definitely dealing with a female entity of some kind, but what exactly is she? If we do some digging into the *liyliyth*, the verse in Isaiah only becomes stranger.

Disclaimer: The following idea is not what I personally believe to be true, but is one view regarding *liyliyth* that is very popular in certain groups. Biblical discretion is advised.

There are some students of the Bible that point to the verse in Isaiah as proof of Lilith, whom they believe was Adam's first wife before Eve. There are several versions of the Lilith story, but they all end with her having sex with an angel and giving birth to demons (angel/human hybrids). According to the story, she was banished to the furthest parts of the earth and does nothing but bear demonic offspring every day.

While the above story does not reflect my personal belief on the subject, the reference to sex between a human woman and angels, which leads to demonic offspring, is interesting. This belief is also just one of the two beliefs surrounding the *liyliyth* and it is the second belief that is much more disturbing than Adam having an unfaithful first wife that was sexually attracted to angels. The Lilith legend is usually associated with the Babylonian *lilitu*, which were female spirits that were worshiped through human sacrifice. The earliest known reference to the *lilitu* was found in an incantation (spell) text dating back to 600 BC.[1]

Babylonian Carving of Lilitu

---

[1] Lesses, Rebecca Exe(o)rcising Power: Women as Sorceresses, Exorcists, and Demonesses in Babylonian Jewish Society of Late Antiquity 2001 JAAR Journal of The American Academy of Religion p.343-375

Chapter 2: What Are Angels?

If we take a slight detour into Babylonian belief, we encounter the father of Gilgamesh, known as Lilu. He was known to sexually seduce women in their sleep, which leads many to believe that he may have been an incubus. An incubus was the male counterpart to the female succubus. Both of these spirits were believed to sexually seduce humans while they slept.

> "Still if some are occasionally begotten from demons, it is not from the seed of such demons, nor from their assumed bodies, but from the seed of men taken for the purpose; as when the demon assumes first the form of a woman, and afterwards of a man; just as they take the seed of other things for other generating purposes."[2] – Thomas Aquinas

The above quote from Thomas Aquinas is important because he was an avid believer that demons and fallen angels could not reproduce with humans, but he also believed that it was happening somehow. The best explanation that he could deduce was provided in the above given quote as to how it happened. The Latin Vulgate also has an interesting translation of the word *liyliyth*.

> "et occurrent daemonia onocentauris et pilosus clamabit alter ad alterum ibi cubavit lamia et invenit sibi requiem" — Isaiah 34:14, Vulgate

There are two words that should draw our attention, and the first is *daemonia* (demon). The second word is *lamia*, it is the Latin equivalent to the Hebrew *liyliyth*. In Greek mythology, Lamia was the queen of Libya, and was also a child eating demon.[3] Later legends refer to multiple *lamiae* (plural) in which they are depicted as entities similar to those found in the vampire legend. In fact, the Vulgate was not the only version of the Bible to make a reference to Lamia. Before the King James Version was published in 1611 and changed the translation to screech owl, the word was included in several other English Bibles.

- Wyclif's Bible – 1395
- Bishop's Bible – 1568

---

[2] Aquinus, Thomas (1265-1274), "Summa Theologica", " Summa Theologica
[3] Aristophanes, *The Wasps*, 1177.

- Douay-Rheims Bible – 1582

The King James alteration of the text is just one in a long line of alterations. In fact, this same word has been changed again in several more recent Bible versions.

- ASV – 1901 – Night Monster
- Emphasized Bible – 1902 – Night Specter
- JPS – 1917 – Night Monster
- Moffatt Translation – 1922 – Vampire
- Jerusalem Bible – 1966 – Lilith
- NRSV – 1989 - Lilith
- MSG – 1993 - Lilith
- NASB – 1995 – Night Monster

The general consensus among Bible translators, historians, mythology, legends, and the meaning of the Hebrew word, is that the *liyliyth* is not an owl as presented in the King James Version. However, as we see in the picture above, the owl was associated with *lilitu*. Keep in mind that we are not talking about modern day, Westernized, movie monsters. Isaiah 34 came from the mouth of God, and it is He that references an entity that was believed by several ancient cultures to be very real and was worshiped through human sacrifice. This may also ultimately explain the origin of pagan goddesses and provide a much needed Biblical explanation to the issue.

It is important that we make an attempt to understand what Isaiah 34:14 is really referring to because the entire chapter is an end time prophecy. In verse 14 alone God makes a reference to wild beasts of the island, satyrs, and a evil female being inhabiting places on earth. If the *liyliyth* or *lamia* will be present on earth in during the last days, it may add one more disturbing aspect to Jesus' statement concerning the end of the age:

> "Men's hearts failing them for fear, and for looking after those things which are coming on the earth: for the powers of heaven shall be shaken." – Luke 21:26

While the above verse does not specifically refer to the *liyliyth*, it may include more than we can imagine at the moment. Verses like Isaiah 34:14 are just one more reason we need to seriously consider what spiritual warfare is and how we engage in it. This brings us to other non-angelic spirits mentioned in the Bible.

Non Angelic Spirits

This is where we go another step beyond the traditional teaching on the spiritual realm, and into the land of the vastly unexplored. In church we are generally taught that God's entire creation includes the following beings:

- God
- Jesus
- Holy Spirit
- Humans
- Angels
- Demons
- Animals

When we take a closer look at scripture, there are certain circumstances in which the spirit being referred to is never classified as an angel, demon, or other. The default assumption is usually to classify all spirits, except for the Holy Spirit, as angels or demons.

> "And there came forth a spirit, and stood before the LORD, and said, I will persuade him." - 1 Kings 22:21

This particular spirit is never identified as an angel or demon. Another strange fact about this event is that this spirit volunteers to be a lying spirit in the mouth of the prophets. The words *elohim* and *mal'ak* are used to refer to angels in the Old Testament, but the word used here is *ruach*.

Opinion: The Bible seems to be pointing to the possibility that all angels and demons are spirits, but not all spirits are angels or demons.

If the above passage was the only one like it in scripture we could simply write it off as an anomaly, but there is another section of scripture that describes four spirit chariots pulled by different color horses.

> "And I turned, and lifted up mine eyes, and looked, and, behold, there came four chariots out from between two mountains; and the mountains were mountains of brass. In the first chariot were red horses; and in the second chariot black horses; And in the third chariot white horses; and in the fourth chariot grisled and bay horses. Then I answered and said unto the angel that talked with me, What are these, my lord? And the angel answered and said unto me, These are the four spirits of the heavens, which go forth from standing before the LORD of all the earth." - Zechariah 6:1-5

In these scriptures, the chariots (*merkabah*) and their horses are clearly referred to as spirits. These four horses are very similar to John's vision of the four horsemen in Revelation 6. As we continue building the case for spirits that are not angels or demons, we encounter another portion of scripture which makes a clear differentiation between the two.

> "And there arose a great cry: and the scribes that were of the Pharisees' part arose, and strove, saying, We find no evil in this man: but if **a spirit or an angel** hath spoken to him, let us not fight against God." - Acts 23:9

Here the scribes stand up in defense of the gospel and make a clear distinction between spirits and angels. The phrase "let us not fight against God" seems to indicate that these spirits are not demons. If they are not demons and they are not angels, what are they? Jesus actually gives us some insight into what a spirit is:

> "But they were terrified and affrighted, and supposed that they had seen a spirit. And he said unto them, Why are ye troubled? and why do thoughts arise in your hearts? Behold my hands and my feet, that it is I myself: handle me, and see; for a spirit hath not flesh and bones, as ye see me have." - Luke 24:39

According to Jesus, spirits do not have flesh and bone, but Jesus did. He did not say there is no such thing as spirits or dismiss spirits as figments of the disciples' imaginations. Instead He told them that spirits are something different than what He is. This brings us to the subject of ghosts. Do humans

Chapter 2: What Are Angels?

come back from the dead as spirits that are responsible for haunting various places around the world?

The Haunted History of Mankind

Throughout history people have been reporting encounters with spirits that seem to manifest, disappear, taunt, and torment them seemingly without reason. Unfortunately, good Biblical explanations are few and far between, and even most of those are only available if we know where to look. Our society seems to have an obsession with communicating with the supernatural realm, which is a very dangerous practice. Believe it or not the Bible has a lot to say about the subject of ghosts, poltergeists, and other hauntings.

> "In thoughts from the visions of the night, when deep sleep falleth on men, Fear came upon me, and trembling, which made all my bones to shake. Then a spirit passed before my face; the hair of my flesh stood up: It stood still, but I could not discern the form thereof: an image was before mine eyes, there was silence, and I heard a voice, saying, Shall mortal man be more just than God? shall a man be more pure than his maker?" – Job 4:13-17

Many believe that Job's encounter was with an angel, some believe that it was with the Holy Spirit, and others believe Job's encounter is Biblical evidence of ghosts. In the story, Job experiences several things that are usually associated with a haunting:

1. He first feels fear.
2. He started to tremble.
3. A spirit manifests.
4. The hair on his body stood up.
5. The spirit had no shape.

If we compare this story with the stories of angelic encounters, they are only similar in two of the five aspects. Angelic encounters usually result in fear and trembling. If we compare this story to the disciples encounter with the resurrected Christ, there is no fear before they see Him, and He also has a definite shape.

"According to the records of the time, they would appear in numerous guises, often as an animal, but also at times as a human or humanoid figure, and were described as "clearly defined, three-dimensional... forms, vivid with colour and animated with movement and sound" by those alleging to have come into contact with them, unlike later descriptions of ghosts with their "smoky, undefined forms".[4]

According to the above statement, formless ghosts are a later description of these ghostly appearances; however, the book of Job is believed to predate Genesis, which was written around 1400BC. There are many scholars that believe that Job was written 2000BC - 1800BC, which would make this encounter over 4,000 years old. This manifestation is only one type of strange encounters in the Bible between people and spirits, but there is another more disturbing practice that was going on in Biblical times and has carried on into modern society.

Talking To The Dead

In our modern times talking to the dead has become a very popular subject in the media. On any given day of the week we can turn on the television and find one or more of the following shows:

1. Ghost Hunters
2. Ghost Adventures
3. Medium
4. Ghost Whisperer
5. Many More

All of these shows have one thing in common: They all encourage communication with the dead. In addition to these shows, there are people like John Edwards and Silvia Brown that make a living by claiming to talk to the dead, but where does this idea of talking to the dead originate? Many people believe that the practice started in Biblical times, but that is not the case.

---

[4] Wilby, Emma (2005). *Cunning Folk and Familiar Spirits: Shamanistic Visionary Traditions in Early Modern British Witchcraft and Magic.* Brighton: Sussex Academic Press.

Chapter 2: What Are Angels?

> "In European folklore and folk-belief of the Medieval and Early Modern periods, familiar spirits, sometimes referred to simply as familiars, were supernatural entities that were believed to assist witches and cunning folk in their practice of magic."[5]

The Bible contains very specific laws concerning talking to the dead, but the idea does not originate in the Bible. The practice of Necromancy (spirit divination) or having a familiar spirit dates all the way back to Babylon. Babylonian Necromancers were referred to as *Manzazuu* and the spirits they raised were referred to as *Etemmu* and *Gidim*. Before we continue it is important to differentiate between these two types of spirits.

> ***Etemmu*** – They were the ghosts of people not properly buried, thus being denied entry to the underworld and doomed to wander the world for all eternity. They are also vengeful towards the living. In modern times these would be what we would refer to as ghosts or poltergeists.

> ***Gidim*** – They are the equivalent of ghosts, but the difference between them and the *Etemmu* is that they were the spirits of dead people living in the Underworld.

Once we dig into the subject of talking to the dead, we can clearly see that the entities that the Babylonians claimed to have contact with were not the same. These entities had different functions and they abode in two different locations. There also seems to be a difference in interpretation as to what these entities are. From a Biblical perspective, only demons and fallen angels are vengeful toward mankind, while the Babylonians held a completely different belief. Let's look at a story in the Bible that is very similar to the belief in the *Gidim*.

> "Now Samuel was dead, and all Israel had lamented him, and buried him in Ramah, even in his own city. And Saul had put away those that had familiar spirits, and the wizards, out of the land." – 1 Samuel 28:3

---

[5] Wilby, Emma (2005). *Cunning Folk and Familiar Spirits: Shamanistic Visionary Traditions in Early Modern British Witchcraft and Magic*. Brighton: Sussex Academic Press.

This is the beginning of Saul's eventual dabbling into the forbidden practice of necromancy. Samuel is dead, God is not speaking to Saul, and the prophets are not speaking to Saul on God's behalf. Saul has also had all of the mediums (those with familiar spirits) and wizards removed from the land. Saul's problem is that he wants to communicate with God, but he cannot go through the established means of communication, which were through himself, Urim, or the other prophets (1 Samuel 28:6). Because of his situation Saul decides to attempt to reach God by forbidden means:

> "Then said Saul unto his servants, Seek me a woman that hath a familiar spirit, that I may go to her, and enquire of her. And his servants said to him, Behold, there is a woman that hath a familiar spirit at Endor." - 1 Samuel 28:7

If we read the above verse very carefully there are a few things that should stand out:

- Saul specifically requests a woman with a familiar spirit.
- Saul believes that this woman is capable of contacting the spirits.
- Saul's servants already know where to find a woman with a familiar spirit.

Why didn't Saul seek out a man with a familiar spirit? Traditionally it was a way of separating the male practitioners from the female practitioners of necromancy. In today's terminology it is similar to calling women witches and men warlocks. As we can see, witchcraft has its origins in the ancient practice of necromancy.

> "And Saul disguised himself, and put on other raiment, and he went, and two men with him, and they came to the woman by night: and he said, I pray thee, divine unto me by the familiar spirit, and bring me him up, whom I shall name unto thee. And the woman said unto him, Behold, thou knowest what Saul hath done, how he hath cut off those that have familiar spirits, and the wizards, out of the land: wherefore then layest thou a snare for my life, to cause me to die? And Saul sware to her by the LORD, saying, As the LORD liveth, there shall no punishment happen to thee for this thing." - 1 Samuel 28:8-10

Chapter 2: What Are Angels?

Saul specifically goes in disguise at night to seek the services of this witch, but she refuses to help him at first. Once Saul promises that she will not be punished, the woman proceeds to pierce the veil between the physical world and the spiritual world. Was she faking it or can the spiritual realm be accessed while we are still in the flesh?

> "Early necromancy is likely related to shamanism, which calls upon spirits such as the ghosts of ancestors. Classical necromancers addressed the dead in "a mixture of high-pitch squeaking and low droning", comparable to the trance-state mutterings of shamans."[6]

While the use of sound to invoke a spiritual response goes far beyond the scope of this book, it was a common practice in ancient times. Certain sounds and tones were believed to attract spirits and certain tones were believed to repel them. We find one such example of a spirit being repelled by David through the playing of music.

> "And it came to pass, when the evil spirit from God was upon Saul, that David took an harp, and played with his hand: so Saul was refreshed, and was well, and the evil spirit departed from him." - 1 Samuel 16:23

While this does not prove beyond a shadow of a doubt that witches can conjure up spirits through vocal sounds, it does give some credibility to the belief in using music to influence a desired response from spirits. However the conjuring of spirits was accomplished, the Bible has very strict warnings concerning those that seek people that engage in the practice.

> "And the soul that turneth after such as have familiar spirits, and after wizards, to go a whoring after them, I will even set my face against that soul, and will cut him off from among his people." - Leviticus 20:6

The consequences for being guilty by association were to be cut off from everything you knew and left to fend for yourself. If you think that is harsh, the penalty for actually being a

---

[6] Luck, Georg (2006). *Arcana Mundi: Magic and the Occult in the Greek and Roman Worlds* (Second Edition). The Johns Hopkins University Press: Baltimore

witch, wizard, or warlock was death (Exodus 22:18). God does not take dabbling into the spiritual realm lightly. The fact is that people do not come back from the dead as spirits to physically manifest and interact with mankind without being conjured up through forbidden ritual, which means that these modern spiritual encounters have to be manifestations of something other than dead humans. However, there is one exception to this rule.

The Exception To The Rule

Jesus seems to be the exception to the rules that human spirits do not come back from the dead on their own and the certainly do not cross over to the spiritual realm while being alive. John 1:32 tells us that we do not know exactly what Jesus became, but whatever it was, we will be just like Him when we are changed.

> **Opinion:** I suspect that Jesus was as Adam was before the fall. He did things that only angels and spirits were known to do, but He was also fully human at the same time. According to Matthew 1:18, Jesus was part human and part Holy Spirit, which is what Christians become after we are saved.

Jesus was a historical and spiritual anomaly. Previous to Christ, only angels could move freely between the physical and spiritual realms under their own power. Jesus was the first person to ever die, come back, and then go back to the spirit realm to present Himself to God, all under His own accord. Even the angels seemed to be baffled by this spiritual anomaly.

> "Searching what, or what manner of time the Spirit of Christ which was in them did signify, when it testified beforehand the sufferings of Christ, and the glory that should follow. Unto whom it was revealed, that not unto themselves, but unto us they did minister the things, which are now reported unto you by them that have preached the gospel unto you with the Holy Ghost sent down from heaven; which things the angels desire to look into." - 1 Peter 1:12

Angels desire to look into or investigate the entire matter of Christ, the Holy Ghost, and the glory that followed His suffering. It is entirely possible that the angels did not fully understand what was going to happen. In fact, scripture seems to indicate that only two angels had access to future information before it was revealed to the prophets.

> "But I will shew thee that which is noted in the scripture of truth: and there is none that holdeth with me in these things, but Michael your prince." - Daniel 10:21

Some people believe that this being was Christ and some believe it was Gabriel, which either way lacks importance. What is important is that at the time, only two beings in the entire universe (not counting God) knew what was going to happen concerning the Holy Spirit, Christ, and mankind.

The Breakdown

Angels seem to be a combination of the physical and the spiritual, and not just one or the other. When Christ came back from the dead He exhibited abilities similar to the angels, and according to scripture, believers will become something similar to what He is. The spiritual realm seems to be much more complex than many of us give it credit for. There does not seem to be a cut and dry answer that will allow us to make a blanket statement over all creation. Anyone pretending to know the full extent of what angels are capable of are lying to themselves and anyone listening. When someone says angels definitely cannot have sex, it is implying that they have full knowledge of angelic physiology, because the Bible never makes such a statement. When someone says that the angels in the Old Testament were just apparitions or only appeared to manifest, they are not sticking to the Biblical text. While we may not find all of the answers about the spiritual realm in the Bible, it is important not to turn our assumptions into doctrine in order to make them fit our preconceived notions.

Chapter in Review

- When were angels created?

- Where do angels fit into history?
- What are angels?
- Do dead people turn into angels?
- How many different spirits are mentioned in the Bible?
- Does the Bible mention female spirits?
- Is it OK to try to contact the dead?

Critical Thinking

- Does the Bible tell us when angels were created?
- Does the Bible tell us what angels are?
- What happens after we die?
- Is it really possible to contact the dead?

The Plan of Salvation

The plan of salvation is not difficult or complicated at all. In fact it can be summed up in one single verse. All you need to do in order to be saved is the following:

> That if thou shalt confess with thy mouth the Lord Jesus, and shalt believe in thine heart that God hath raised him from the dead, thou shalt be saved." – Romans 10:9

If you have accepted Christ, your next step should be to get your hands on a King James Version of the Bible. Before joining any church, you should have a good foundation in scripture without the influences of any teacher. Once you have a general understanding of scripture, visit a few churches before deciding on a church home. Make sure you check behind the pastor and do not just accept their word for anything without checking (Acts 17:11). If asking questions is discouraged, steer clear of that church at all costs.

Key Scriptures For Review

- Genesis 5
- Leviticus 20

Chapter 2: What Are Angels?

- Numbers 27
- 1 Samuel 16
- 1 Samuel 28
- 1 Kings 22
- Job 4
- Job 38
- Psalms 8
- Isaiah 14
- Isaiah 34
- Daniel 9
- Daniel 10
- Zechariah 5
- Zechariah 6
- Luke 21
- Luke 24
- John 1
- Acts 16
- Acts 23
- Romans 8
- 1 Corinthians 6
- 1 Corinthians 15
- Hebrews 2
- Hebrews 13
- 1 Peter 1

Submit Your Questions

If you have more questions about spiritual warfare, angels, demons, the supernatural, or the Bible in general, you are welcome to submit your questions to me personally. Answers to your questions will be posted as an article on the website for everyone to see.

www.MinisterFortson.com

Chapter 3: The Ranks of Angels

> "We are locked in a battle. This is not a friendly, gentleman's discussion. It is a life and death conflict between the spiritual hosts of wickedness and those who claim the name of Christ." – Francis A Schaeffer

One indication of free will and intelligence is the ability to organize and separate things into groups; we find this in the Bible in reference to angel society. The term "ranks" can be a little misleading because it implies a specific chain of command. For example, Lucifer is a Cherub, but only one of five mentioned in scripture. It is traditionally believed that Lucifer once led all the angels of heaven. On the other hand, Michael is referred to as an archangel, yet he currently leads the army of heaven. If the rank of Cherub is higher than archangel, then the four Cherubim seen around the throne of God would be leading the army of heaven, with Michael being second in command or even further down the chain of command. Because we do not see this in the Bible, it is important that we understand what the ranks of angels are all about.

Traditional Christian Hierarchy

Rank	Good	Bad
Seraphim	X	X
Cherubim	X	X
Thrones/Ophanim	X	X
Dominions	X	X
Virtues	X	X
Powers	X	X
Principalities	X	X
Archangels	X	X
Angels	X	X

Traditional Jewish Hierarchy

Rank	Good	Bad
Chayot	X	-
Ophanim	X	-
Erelim	X	-

Chapter 3: The Ranks of Angels

Hashmallim	X	-
Seraphim	X	-
Malakim	X	-
Elohim	X	X
Bene Elohim	X	X
Cherubim	X	X
Ishim	X	X

The first thing we notice is that the traditional Jewish hierarchy contains more ranks than the traditional Christian hierarchy, and some of the names are completely different than those we are familiar with. In this chapter we are going to attempt to understand the various ranks of angels and the roles they play in spiritual warfare.

Understanding The Hierarchy

There are a lot of misconceptions when it comes to angels and their ranks. Some churches teach that Gabriel and Lucifer are archangels even though the Bible never refers to either of them as such. These are just two misconceptions that are commonly made about angels, but are not backed by scripture. For the purposes of this chapter, the word "angel" is used solely as an all encompassing word to describe all spiritual beings except for demons.

Theory: The angelic hierarchy or types of angels are more of a references to different races or types of angels. Much like people are referred to as African, European, Spanish, etc.

Archangels, Rulers and Principalities: When we think of Archangels, Rulers and Principalities, we usually associate Archangels with being the good guys, and Rulers and Principalities are usually associated with being the bad guys. Because of this clear separation, it is often assumed that these are angels of different ranks. However, when we do a comparative study of the words, we find the following:

- *Archo Aggelos* (Archangels) - Archo is a Greek verb meaning "to rule".

- *Arche* (Principalities) – Also a Greek word meaning, "to rule".
- *Kosmokratór* (Rulers)– A Greek word meaning, "world ruler"

It is important to point out that some researchers believe that Rulers and Principalities are the same type of angel. For the purpose of this section, we will be referring to both as Principalities. The Greek origin of both words is *archomai*, meaning "to rule" or "commence". When we examine the origin of both words, what we seem to have are the same type of angels, but on opposite sides of the battlefield. If we refer to the above traditional ranking order, it would appear that Principalities are outranked by Archangels, but that does not seem to be the case because Principalities do not answer to the angels on God's side. This is one indication that what we refer to as a rank, may actually be a type, race, or species of angel.

Powers: It is believed by some that the Powers are the bearers of conscience and keepers of history. While this is merely speculation, the Bible does make mention of them having a prince over them. The term "prince" is used in the Bible many times to refer to angelic beings:

> "Wherein in time past ye walked according to the course of this world, according to the prince of the power of the air, the spirit that now worketh in the children of disobedience:" – Ephesians 2:2

- **Powers** - *Exousia* – A Greek word meaning, "authority, weight, influence, delegated power".

It is important to point out that the above verse could also simply refer to the angel that has power of the air, such as those in Revelation 7:1. This brings us to the rank of angels known as the Thrones.

Thrones: There is not much in the Bible as far as information on the Thrones; most of the beliefs surrounding these beings come from Jewish tradition and not scripture.

Chapter 3: The Ranks of Angels

- **Thrones/Ophanim** - *Thronos* – A Greek word meaning, "power, a stately seat, potentate".

In Ezekiel 1, we encounter "Ezekiel's Wheels". Many people have speculated as to what he actually saw. Some believe that he saw the throne of God, chariots of heaven, or a UFO. While there are some that view these "wheels" as non living objects, according to Ezekiel, they have a spirit inside of them:

> "Whithersoever the spirit was to go, they went, thither was their spirit to go; and the wheels were lifted up over against them: for the spirit of the living creature was in the wheels."
> – Ezekiel 1:20

The text is not clear as to whether the living creatures are controlling the wheels or if the wheels are controlling the living creatures. What we do know is that they moved as a single unit. This brings us to the final two groups of angels.

- **Dominions** - *Kuriotes* – A Greek word meaning, "angelic lordship, dignity, government".
- **Angels** – *Aggelos* – A Greek word meaning "messenger".

The Bible does not have much to say about Dominions, but on the other hand it has a lot to say about angels. The *aggelos* are what we see all throughout both the Old and New Testaments, and we will learn more about them later in this chapter. Now that we have somewhat of an understanding of the traditional ranking of angels, we will take a little bit deeper look into some of the more complicated and lesser taught areas of the angelic hierarchy.

Lesser Known Terminology

Sometimes, we as Christians get so wrapped up in our own theology that we forget that the Bible is a Jewish text. While we may be familiar with some common Hebrew terminology such as the words Torah, YHVH/YHWH, and Bethel, there are many other words we need to be aware of as well. Having knowledge of some of these lesser known terms may provide many other insights that are commonly overlooked.

> *Chay* – In Ezekiel 1, this word is translated as "living creatures". Many researchers believe that the chay, cherubim, and seraphim are the same type of spiritual being.
>
> *Ophanim* – The Ophanim are known as the "many eyed ones", and are usually associated with Ezekiel's Wheels (Ezekiel 1:15-21). These are believed to be the literal wheels of God's chariot (*merkabah*).
>
> *Bene Elohim* – This term is used in Genesis 6, Job 1,2, and 38 to refer to angels. In the 3rd century, Sextus Julius Africanus began promoting the completely twisted interpretation that refers to them as the "sons of Seth", even though the name Seth is never mentioned in the text.

It is important to familiarize ourselves with these less than familiar terms because they are used in the Bible over and over again. These terms will also lay the foundation for many of the strange beings we will encounter as we travel through scripture. Some examples are the references to certain angels being referred to as royalty.

The Royal Group of Angels

Throughout the Bible, angels are also referred to as princes, kings, and gods. Ironically, many churches teach that gods of pagan cultures were not real, even though the Bible verifies their existence on at least two occasions. Although this is the case, not all angels are referred to as princes, kings, or gods. These titles seem to be reserved for a select group of beings that have a higher position of authority.

- Prince of Persia (Daniel 10:13)
- Prince of Greece (Daniel 10:20)
- Prince of Israel (Daniel 12:1)
- Prince of the Power of The Air (Ephesians 2:2)
- Prince of Devils (Matthew 12:24)
- The Fallen Princes (Psalm 82:7)
- King of The Locusts (Revelation 9:11)

The Biblical use of this term usually refers to a spiritual being that has control over a specific territory. The angel Gabriel fought with one of these princes while trying to reach Daniel, and according to the story he needed Michael's help to prevail.

> "But the prince of the kingdom of Persia withstood me one and twenty days: but, lo, Michael, one of the chief princes, came to help me; and I remained there with the kings of Persia." - Daniel 10:13

In Daniel 10:13, Michael is referred to as one of the "chief princes". As we have encountered several times in the KJV, the translation of the word does not convey the complete line of thought behind it. In this particular case, the word that does not come across fully is the word "chief". The Hebrew word used for "chief" is *rishon*. It can also mean "first, oldest, ancestors, or earlier". The choice of wording here seems to imply age and not necessarily the level of authority. This is important because it points to one or both of the two following possibilities:

1. Some angels are older than others.
2. Some angels have held positions of power longer than others.

Either one or both of these could be true. If the first statement is true, then all of the angels were not created at the same time. If the second statement is true, not all angels were appointed or obtained high positions of power at the same time.

Opinion: If the Hebrew word *rishon* points to either the first or second statement above as being true, it adds a completely new layer of mystery and complexity to what we as Christians know about angels and their civilization.

Many cultures around the world also express this same line of thinking in regards to princes from the sky and the gods that were created, but not necessarily at the same time. Some have translated the Babylonian word *Anunnaki* to mean: "Those of princely origin". In my book, <u>As The Days of Noah Were</u>, there is a detailed comparison that shows the similarities between the legend of the *Anunnaki* rebellion and what we Christians refer to as Satan's rebellion. What Christians must absolutely deal with is the fact that much of what we refer to as mythology actually agrees with what the Bible is saying.

Of Gods and Messengers

One of the interesting classifications that we run across in the Bible is the distinction between the gods and the angels. Sometimes the word "gods" is used to refer to idols, but other times it is used to refer very real supernatural beings. In order to understand the differentiation between the gods and the messengers, we are going to look at four words. Two of them are in Hebrew and two of them are in Greek.

The first Hebrew word is:

> *Elohim* (Strong's #430) - This word is always translated in one of two ways in the Bible: God (singular) or gods (plural). The choice of translation is usually based on whether or not the word *Elohim* appears with a singular or a plural verb. In many versions of the *Tanakh* (Hebrew Old Testament) the word *Elohim* is translated as "divine being".

The word "divine" is usually attributed to God, which confuses many people when the word is used to refer to something other than the God of the Bible. There are close to twenty definitions for the word divine, but we are only going to look at four of those in order to demonstrate why angels are referred to as divine beings. These four definitions will consist of two adjectives, one noun, and one verb. Pay close attention to the following definitions because they will become more important as we proceed through the rest of the book.

Adjective Definition #1: "Being godlike or having characteristics befitting of a deity."

Adjective Definition #2: "heavenly or celestial"

Noun Definition #1: The spiritual aspect of humans. A group of attributes and qualities of humankind regarded as godly or godlike.

Verb Definition #1: To discover or declare something obscure or in the future by divination. It also means to prophesy.

As we see from the definitions above, the word divine does not only refer to God or goodness, but it also refers to having characteristics usually attributed to a deity. When the word *elohim* is used to refer to angels, it is describing beings that are similar to God in characteristics, but not equal to God. One place that we see this demonstrated in the Bible is in Psalm 82:1:

> "God standeth in the congregation of the mighty; he judgeth among the gods." - Psalm 82:1

The Hebrew translation actually conveys a much deeper meaning. God is standing in judgment among the gods or in other words, those with attributes like Him, but not equal to Him. A second scripture that uses the word *elohim* in reference to beings that are like God, but not God Himself, is in 1 Samuel 28:12. This is what the witch of Endor saw while trying to communicate with the dead prophet Samuel.

> "And the king said unto her, Be not afraid: for what sawest thou? And the woman said unto Saul, I saw gods ascending out of the earth." - 1 Samuel 28:13

If you were raised in a Christian household or church, chances are you were taught that the gods that were worshiped by other cultures were nothing more than lifeless idols. There are many researchers that believe that the idols were just visual representations of real entities that were being worshipped by these pagan cultures.

Stone Carving of Winged Gods

The above picture is just one of many carvings that we find in the ancient world of winged beings worshiped as the gods. The similarity to the Biblical description of winged angels leads many researchers to believe that the gods were indeed fallen angels interfering in the affairs of mankind.

The second Hebrew word is:

> Mal'ak - This word can mean: "messenger of God, ambassador of God, or deputy of God", but is usually translated in the KJV as "angel".

We usually see this term when "the angel of the Lord" appears or angels on a special mission from God appear. The first example of the use of the word *mal'ak* comes from Genesis 28:12:

> "And he dreamed, and behold a ladder set up on the earth, and the top of it reached to heaven: and behold the angels of God ascending and descending on it." – Genesis 28:12

This dream is commonly referred to as "Jacob's Ladder". Notice that Jacob's vision is very similar to what the Witch of Endor saw in 1 Samuel 28:13. The big difference here is that the witch saw *elohim* and Jacob saw *mal'ak*. There were several differences between what the witch saw and what Jacob saw. The witch saw beings with Godlike characteristics, moving between earth and the underworld, only after attempting to make contact with the spiritual realm. Jacob saw ambassadors of God, moving between heaven and earth, while receiving a vision from God. These are examples of two completely different types of contact with beings we refer to as angels. The second example of the use of the word *mal'ak* comes from Genesis 19:1:

> "And there came two angels to Sodom at even; and Lot sat in the gate of Sodom: and Lot seeing them rose up to meet them; and he bowed himself with his face toward the ground;" - Genesis 19:1

These two angels were originally part of a trio that came to visit Abraham on the plain. One of the angels stayed behind, and Abraham referred to him as the "Judge of all the earth". The two angels referred to in Genesis 19:1 continued on to Sodom, in order to judge whether or not they would destroy the five cities on the plain.

The reason we need to be aware of the difference between the use of the word *elohim* and the use of the word *mal'ak*, in reference to angels is because it seems to differentiate the good angels from the fallen angels. If we take a very critical look at the Bible, we notice that there seems to be a lack of information about fallen angels. However, when we look at the Hebrew terminology used to refer to the gods, that misconception changes. The Bible says a lot about the activity of fallen angels on earth. Many of the human interactions with fallen angels were written and carved by almost every culture on earth.

Psalm 82 and Genesis 19 also convey the point that there is a difference between the *mal'ak* and the *elohim*. In Psalm 82, we see God standing in judgment of the *elohim*, but in Genesis 19, we see the *mal'ak* sent to hand out judgment from God. Based on the text, the *elohim* seem to have done something worthy of God's judgment and according to Psalm 82:7 they will die like men (*Adam*) and fall like one of the princes.

> **Theory:** Based on the context in which the words *elohim* and *mal'ak* are used in the Bible, the *elohim* seem to be the bad guys (fallen angels) and the *mal'ak* seem to be the good guys (angels of God).

This differentiation between the two groups may also provide a little more insight into what Satan was talking about in the Garden of Eden.

> "For God doth know that in the day ye eat thereof, then your eyes shall be opened, and ye shall be as gods, knowing good and evil." – Genesis 3:5

In this verse the word *elohim* is translated once as God and once as gods. Many pastors will wrongly quote the above verse and change gods to God in order to push the belief that there are no gods. If this theory is true, Adam and Eve not only became like the gods in the sense of knowing good from evil, they also became like the gods in the sense that they also became fallen, disobedient, and rebellious creations of God.

The Greek words we are going to look at are:

- *Theos* – This Greek word is translated in the New Testament as God or gods.
- *Aggelos* - This Greek word is translated in the New Testament as angel, but literally means "messenger".

The word *theos* is rarely used to refer to anything other than God and idols. The New Testament writers just come right out and refer to all heavenly beings as angels, whether they are good or bad. Without repeating all of the above information, the Greek word *aggelos* is used in the same manner in which *mal'ak* and *elohim* are used in Hebrew.

> "But though we, or an angel from heaven, preach any other gospel unto you than that which we have preached unto you, let him be accursed." – Galatians 1:8

Here Paul uses the word *aggelos* to refer to fallen angels potentially preaching a false gospel. Only fallen angels would preach an entirely different gospel than that which is presented in the Bible. Mormonism and Islam are just two of many religions that claim to have been handed down by angels that

Chapter 3: The Ranks of Angels

were preaching a strange gospel. Any religion that contradicts the Bible and has its origins from an angel or a being from the sky should be avoided. Paul also alludes to the traditional teaching of Genesis 6 in 1 Corinthians 11:10, a tradition that points to the women's hair as the reason the angels began to lust after them. The following translation of the Testament of Reuben (not scripture) confirms what Paul says about women's hair:

> "... flee from sexual promiscuity, and order your wives and your daughters not to adorn their heads and their appearances so as to deceive men's sound minds. For every woman who schemes in these ways is destined for eternal punishment. **For it was thus that they charmed the Watchers, who were before the Flood. As they continued looking at the women, they were filled with desire for them and perpetrated the act in their minds.** Then they were transformed into human males, and while the women were cohabiting with their husbands they appeared to them. Since the women's minds were filled with lust for these apparitions, they gave birth to giants. For the Watchers were disclosed to them as being as high as the heavens." - Translation of the Testament of Reuben by H. C. Keein James H. Charlesworth (1983-1985): v. 1, p. 784

The New Testament, especially the writings of Paul, reflects many long held beliefs surrounding both good and bad angels. This is just one more reason that we as Christians need to be aware of both Jewish tradition and Jewish terminology.

The Breakdown

Both the Bible and history are filled with references to beings that were created by God, but later chose to rebel or stay and serve Him. Sadly, Church tradition has hindered the in depth study of some of the topics presented in this chapter. It is my opinion that many of the traditions in Church need to be challenged with scripture. If they do not stand up in the face of clear Biblical text, they need to be disregarded altogether. It is also my opinion that angelology and demonology as it is taught in mainstream churches needs a drastic upgrade from many of the archaic and completely false ideas that have been passed on from pastor to pastor without being questioned.

The angelic hierarchy seems to be very well thought out and more complex than we give it credit for. Much of it is still a mystery and many questions about it are not answered in the Bible. We do not know if it was established by God or by the angels themselves. Perhaps we are not supposed to know this information because the focus of the Bible is on spiritual warfare, redemption through Christ, and God's love for mankind. Whatever the reason, the fact remains that angelic society is a fascinating study.

Chapter in Review

- Does the Christian hierarchy of angels match the Jewish hierarchy of angels?
- Are there references to other kinds of angels in the Hebrew text?
- Are angels ever referred to as royalty?
- Are good and bad angels referred to by different terms in the Bible?

Critical Thinking

- Does the hierarchy of angels refer to their level of importance or something else?
- What are the additional ranks of angels in the Hebrew text?
- Why would angels be referred to as princes and kings?
- Are the gods of mythology really stories about fallen angels?

The Plan of Salvation

The plan of salvation is not difficult or complicated at all. In fact it can be summed up in one single verse. All you need to do in order to be saved is the following:

> That if thou shalt confess with thy mouth the Lord Jesus, and shalt believe in thine heart that God hath raised him from the dead, thou shalt be saved." - Romans 10:9

Chapter 3: The Ranks of Angels

If you have accepted Christ, your next step should be to get your hands on a King James Version of the Bible. Before joining any church, you should have a good foundation in scripture without the influences of any teacher. Once you have a general understanding of scripture, visit a few churches before deciding on a church home. Make sure you check behind the pastor and do not just accept their word for anything without checking (Acts 17:11). If asking questions is discouraged, steer clear of that church at all costs.

Key Scriptures For Review

- Genesis 3
- Genesis 19
- Genesis 28
- 1 Samuel 28
- Psalm 82
- Ezekiel 1
- Daniel 10
- Galatians 1
- Ephesians 2

Submit Your Questions

If you have more questions about spiritual warfare, angels, demons, the supernatural, or the Bible in general, you are welcome to submit your questions to me personally. Answers to your questions will be posted as an article on the website for everyone to see.

www.MinisterFortson.com

Angels 102: A Supernatural Society

Chapter 4: Rise of An Adversary

"Be extremely subtle even to the point of formlessness. Be extremely mysterious even to the point of soundlessness. Thereby you can be the director of the opponent's fate." — Sun Tzu, The Art of War

The idea of studying the Devil is considered taboo in many Christian churches. Often times he is displayed in a comical manner as if he is some kind of joke to be taken lightly. However, we are in a war and we cannot recognize your enemy if we do not know anything about our enemy. The Devil is probably the most misunderstood being in the Bible, and because of this, many Christians have no idea who he is or what his ultimate goal is. The goal of this chapter is to remove several layers of the veil that are currently over the Church's eyes concerning this former servant of God. Should we as Christians take the Devil seriously or should we continue to ignore what the Bible has to say about our adversary?

What The Devil Is Not

Before defining who and what the Devil is, it is important to define what he is not. There are several religions that claim to be Christians, but at the same time they teach views on the Devil that are not Biblical. Sometimes he is depicted as God's opposite, so let's take a look at three attributes that are commonly used to describe God.

- Omnipotent – All Powerful.
- Omniscient – All Knowing.
- Omnipresent – All Present.

None of the above attributes are ever attributed to the Devil in the Bible, so he cannot be God's opposite. Contrary to popular belief, the Devil is not and cannot be everywhere wreaking havoc on the world at all times. He cannot be two places at once and he is also not some dumb, mindless, spirit that stops our car from working ten minutes before we get to work. When we see him in the Bible, his presence is reserved for special occasions when trying to thwart God's plan.

Who Is The Devil?

In every story there is a protagonist (hero) and an antagonist (villain), and the same applies to the Bible; the Devil and his angels are the villains. When we read the Bible in Hebrew, we discover that every name has a meaning that describes the characteristics of an individual. Let's start by learning the names of the Devil, so we can figure out the characteristics of this being that made himself an enemy of God.

- *Helel* – Shining One (Isaiah 14:12)
- *Ha Satan* - The Adversary (Job 1 & 2)
- *Diablos* – False Accuser, Slanderer (Matthew 4:1)
- *Nakhash* – Serpent/Shining One (Genesis 3:1)
- *Lucifer* – Light Bearer (Isaiah 14:12)
- The Great Red Dragon – Revelation 12:3
- King of Tyrus – Ezekiel 28:12

Based on his names, we know that he is the adversary, the shining one, a false accuser, a slanderer, and the light bearer. Throughout this book, these names will be used interchangeably to refer to the same being. Now that we know his attributes, let's take a more detailed look at what the Bible has to say about his Character, based on his actions.

Helel and Lucifer

Helel is the Hebrew equivalent to the Latin name *Lucifer*. Both of these names mean "light bearer". When we turn to the book of Ezekiel, we find a detailed description of what some believe to be descriptions of light.

> "Thou hast been in Eden the garden of God; every precious stone was thy covering, the sardius, topaz, and the diamond, the beryl, the onyx, and the jasper, the sapphire, the emerald, and the carbuncle, and gold: the workmanship of thy tabrets and of thy pipes was prepared in thee in the day that thou wast created." - Ezekiel 28:13

Chapter 4: Rise of An Adversary

There are some that believe that the stones listed represent various colors of light and not literal stones, but others believe they are simply stones as described. However, there may be a third alternative, and that is that both beliefs may be right. Finely polished stones such as diamonds reflect light, as does gold, and most other metals. These may be literal stones that reflect light in various color spectrums. There may also be another purpose for the above description, but we will explore that later in the chapter.

Although he is called the light bearer, he may not actually be an angel of light. Throughout this book we will refer to Paul because of his insight into the spiritual realm. Paul's comments in 2 Corinthians seem to indicate that the Devil can only pretend to be an angel of light.

> "For such are false apostles, deceitful workers, transforming themselves into the apostles of Christ. And no marvel; for Satan himself is transformed into an angel of light." - 2 Corinthians 11:13-14

The English translation does not seem convey Paul's words as strongly as the Greek does. Paul was addressing the people of the church at Corinth about false leaders in the church. The next part of the text says, "and no marvel", which actually conveys Paul's feelings toward the false apostles. The Greek phrase *kai ou thaumastos* means, "nothing marvelous, nothing special, nothing wonderful." Paul is saying that there is nothing special about these false apostles disguising themselves as genuine apostles. It is the next section of the verse that gives us insight into the angelic realm and why the humanly transformation act is nothing special.

Satan can transform himself into an angel of light, which indicates that he is not actually an angel of light. The Greek word for transform is *metaschématizó*, which means "disguise". While we are on the subject of light, it is necessary to point out that this is only one possible translation of the word. The word used for light in this verse is *phos*, which can also mean: fire. To put this in perspective, the Greek word *phos* is the basis for the word phosphorus, which means "light bringer". In the Septuagint (Greek Bible), the words *Lucifer* and *Helel* in Isaiah 14:12 are translated as *heosphorus* (phosphorus). The reason we need to be aware of this possibility is because as we search the scriptures we do not find any references to angels of light, but we do find an Old Testament reference to "ministers of fire".

> "Who maketh his angels spirits; his ministers a flaming fire:" - Psalm 104:4

In order to really understand what is being said in this verse, we need to understand that the term for angel used in this verse is *malak*, which refers to a "messenger", and not a divine being or heavenly being. As previously mentioned, the term *malak* was reserved for God's personal messengers, but more specifically the angel of the Lord. The latter half of the verse translates the word *sharath* as ministers, but the Hebrew indicates that these are God's personal servants or attendants.

Now this obscure reference to Satan transforming himself into an "angel of light" is starting to become clearer. What this indicates is that Satan can transform himself into a personal messenger of God, similar to how the false apostles pretended to be personal messengers of God. Consider how many religions and denominations have been started because an angel appears and preaches a strange gospel or a person claims to have been sent as a messenger of God. In the Old Testament, God sent His personal angels to convey a message to the prophets. Because many people have not familiarized themselves with their entire Bible, they are deceived into believing that all angels that appear as light are good. Again, we will refer to Paul for a warning about this very deception.

> But though we, or an angel from heaven, preach any other gospel unto you than that which we have preached unto you, let him be accursed." - Galatians 1:8

Why would an angel from heaven preach another gospel? The transformation into an angel of light seems to have a purpose, and seems to be to steer God's people off course. There are three very huge religious deceptions that have occurred so far, based on the appearance of an angel:

- Catholicism
- Islam

Chapter 4: Rise of An Adversary

- Mormonism

All of these people seem to be sincere in what they believe, however, what they believe does not actually line up with what the Bible says. In some cases, parts of their religion are even contrary to what the Bible says. Catholicism has venerated Mary to equal status as Christ although the Bible neither condones nor encourages this. There are statues and rooms with candles specifically made for praying to the dead, which the Bible also condemns. Most of these practices revolve around visions or encounters that some claim to have had with Mary and other spirits of light.

Islam was started when an entity claiming to be the angel Gabriel appeared to Mohammed. According to some sources, Mohammed had to be convinced by his wife that this spirit was not an evil *djinn* before he would believe what it was telling him. Muslims believe that Jesus was a prophet, however, they do not believe He is the Son of God, which is contrary to the gospel. Another telling sign is the widespread hatred of the Jews, which are God's chosen people. It is more than just a coincidence that there is a link between the arrival of an angel, the handing down of a religion that denounces Christ, and teaches hatred of the Jewish nation.

Mormonism was started when Joseph Smith received a vision from the angel Moroni. This angel directed him to a set of golden plates that taught a gospel other than what the Bible teaches. The deeper we dig into the Mormon religion, the more we discover that it has many points that are in direct conflict with the teaching of the Bible. One of these beliefs is that we can eventually become gods. That is the same lie that Satan used in the garden against Eve (Genesis 3), it is the same lie that the people at Babel believed (Genesis 11), and it is the same reason Lucifer wanted to take over heaven (Isaiah 14). In almost every city in America, we can find young men on bikes, spreading the false gospel of Mormonism.

There are many other religions started by beings appearing to people, but Islam, Catholicism, and Mormonism are significant because they are so wide spread and strategically positioned. Catholicism's central location is in Europe, but it is also a very prevalent force in South America. Islam encompasses most of the Middle East, some of Europe, parts of Africa, and parts of the United States. Mormonism is present all over the United States. Europe, the Middle East, and the United States influence the entire world both politically and religiously. There may be something to this scenario or there could be nothing at all, but we should all begin taking a very critical look at what is going on and start asking more questions.

Ha Satan

Ha Satan is Hebrew for the adversary. It seems to be more of a title than an actual name. From the very beginning, Satan sets himself up as the adversary of God and mankind in the Garden of Eden (Genesis 3). It is possible that Satan uses mankind to get back at God since he cannot directly cause harm to Him. There are other passages that refer to Satan actually turning his attention to special situations at certain times in history.

- Temptation of Eve (Genesis 3)
- Stealing the body of Moses (Jude 1:9)
- The torment of Job (Job 1 & 2)
- The temptation of Christ (Matthew 4:1)
- The betrayal of Christ (Luke 22:3)
- The war in heaven with Michael (Revelation 12:7)

When soldiers go to war they do their homework on the enemy. The problem that many Christians face is that we know very little about our enemy, but our enemy knows a lot about us.

> "My people are destroyed for lack of knowledge: because thou hast rejected knowledge, I will also reject thee, that thou shalt be no priest to me: seeing thou hast forgotten the law of thy God, I will also forget thy children." - Isaiah 4:6

Unlike many of us, Satan knows the word of God very well, if not word for word. There are some church leaders that teach that Satan, other fallen angels, and demons cannot read the Bible, but that is absolutely false. On at least two occasions in the Bible, Satan actually quotes God's word, and one time is a direct quote from the mouth of God. Both of those occasions involved the temptation of two very important people.

> "And the LORD God commanded the man, saying, Of every tree of the garden thou mayest freely eat: But of the tree of the knowledge of good and evil, thou shalt not eat of it: for in the day that thou eatest thereof thou shalt surely die." - Genesis 2:16-17

Eve was not created until Genesis 2:21, which means she was not present when God gave this command to Adam. At some point Eve is informed by either God or Adam of the command because it is the basis of her conversation with the serpent. The important thing to take note of is how Satan approached Eve during the temptation.

> "Now the serpent was more subtil than any beast of the field which the LORD God had made. And he said unto the woman, Yea, hath God said, Ye shall not eat of every tree of the garden?" - Genesis 3:1

He starts by asking her if God actually said not to eat from the tree. We do not know exactly who Eve heard it from, but Satan planted a seed of doubt in her head. If he had tempted Adam directly, it is possible that Adam would have said, "yes", and kept on about his walk in the garden, since we know for a fact that Adam heard it directly from the mouth of God. The point is not who Satan decided to tempt, but that Satan did not just show up in the garden quoting a commandment that God gave to Adam. He was somewhere close enough to overhear their conversation because there is nothing in scripture that indicates it was written down anywhere for him to read. In the second occasion he actually quotes several verses from the book of Psalms.

> "And saith unto him, If thou be the Son of God, cast thyself down: for it is written, He shall give his angels charge concerning thee: and in their hands they shall bear thee up, lest at any time thou dash thy foot against a stone." - Matthew 4:6

Just before this temptation, Jesus answered the previous temptation by saying, "it is written". Satan's next attempt was to use the same line of reasoning by telling Jesus, "it is written". Satan can read scripture, but notice that there are two things that Satan neglects to quote from Psalms 91. "to keep thee in all of thy ways" and the very next verse.

> "Thou shalt tread upon the lion and adder: the young lion and the dragon shalt thou trample under feet." - Psalm 91:13

In 1 Peter 5:8 Satan is referred to as a roaring lion. The Hebrew word used in Psalm 91:13 for adder is *pethen*, which means "venomous serpent" and we know that Satan is referred to as a serpent in Genesis 3. Finally Psalm 91:13 speaks of trampling the dragon under His feet. Revelation 12 refers to Satan as the dragon. He tempted Jesus by using the written Word of God, but purposely neglected to mention his own destruction. If Satan knows the Word of God by heart, so should we.

Diablos

There are two words in the Greek that are translated as devil. Those words are *diablos* and *daimon*. One is used as a proper noun (diablos), and the other is used to refer to demons in general (*daimon*). This word *diablos* means "false accuser" or "slanderer". Church tradition teaches that the Devil accuses us day and night before God, based on the following verse.

> "And I heard a loud voice saying in heaven, Now is come salvation, and strength, and the kingdom of our God, and the power of his Christ: for the accuser of our brethren is cast down, which accused them before our God day and night." - Revelation 12:10

The reference to Satan accusing the brethren before God day and night is usually taught as an ongoing accusation, but if that is true, when does he have time to lead his rebellion? The Greek word used is *hemera* (day), which refers to the period between sun up and sun down. The Greek word *nux* is usually used to refer to midnight. If the above is true, our adversary

Chapter 4: Rise of An Adversary

spends at the very least, 50% of his time accusing us before God. When someone makes an accusation, they are usually trying to bring judgment upon the accused if the accusation is truthful. The reason for these accusations seems to be an attempt to provoke God into taking action against us for our sins. Thankfully, Christ's sacrifice on the cross allows us to be spared from God's wrath. This seems to be a "Plan B" which deviates from the original plan of stopping the redemption of mankind.

The Five I Wills

In the book of Isaiah we find out where the rebellion started and according to the text it was not in heaven. Satan's rebellion started long before he started building his army of angels. According to Isaiah 14:13-14, Satan's rebellion started in his heart with five statements:

1. I will ascend into heaven.
2. I will exalt my throne above the stars of God.
3. I will sit upon the mount of the congregation.
4. I will ascend above the heights of the clouds.
5. I will be like the Most High.

The order and wording of the above statements is very interesting, but let's start with a simple question. If Satan was in heaven when he decided to rebel, why did his first statement involve ascending into heaven?

I Will Ascend Into Heaven

If we take the statement in Isaiah at face value, the only thing we can conclude is that Satan had to be somewhere other than heaven. There are many researchers that believe in what is known as the Gap Theory. This is the period of time in which many people believe that Satan's rebellion occurred and it resulted in the destruction of the earth.

In Genesis 1:2, the KJV reads, "the earth was without form and void." However, there are some that believe the word "was" is a mistranslation because of the way the Hebrew word is used. The Hebrew word used is *hayah*, which means "to become" or "became". *Hayah* is the same word translated as "became" in Genesis 19:26 in reference to Lot's wife. The phrase, "without form and void", are the Hebrew words *tohu vavohu*. *Tohu* means "confused" or "ruined" and *vavohu* means "desolate" or "destroyed". The meanings of these words lead some to believe that this is the timeframe in which Lucifer rebelled and fell from heaven.

Job 38:7 tells us that "the sons of God" shouted for joy when the earth was created, so we know that angels were created sometime prior to Genesis 1:1. What happened between the time in Genesis 1:1 and 1:2 that caused the earth to become confused and destroyed? 1 Corinthians 14:33 tells us that God is not the author of confusion, so something or someone else seems to have caused the earth to become confused.

> "For thus saith the LORD that created the heavens; God himself that formed the earth and made it; he hath established it, **he created it not in vain**, he formed it to be inhabited: I am the LORD; and there is none else." - Isaiah 45:18

Here we see that God did not create the earth in "vain". The word translated as vain is the Hebrew word *tohu*. Genesis 1:2 says the earth was *tohu*, which is the same word used in Isaiah 45:18. Paul tells us that God is not the author of confusion and Isaiah tells us that God did not create the earth confused. Are there any clues in the Bible that reveal to us how the earth became confused?

> "I beheld the earth, and, lo, it was without form, and void; and the heavens, and they had no light. I beheld the mountains, and, lo, they trembled, and all the hills moved lightly. I beheld, and, lo, **there was no man**, and all the birds of the heavens were fled. I beheld, and, lo, the fruitful place was a wilderness, and all the cities thereof were broken down at the presence of the LORD, and by his fierce anger." - Jeremiah 4:23-26

Here Jeremiah is viewing the earth as we see in Genesis 1:1, but he adds a few interesting observations.

Chapter 4: Rise of An Adversary

1. The mountains trembled.
2. There was no man.
3. The birds have fled.
4. The fruitful place has become a wilderness.
5. The cities were destroyed.
6. God is angry.

In order to put together the pieces, we first need to ask ourselves if this is consistent with the Genesis account. According to the last part of Genesis 1:2, "darkness" was upon the face of the deep. The Hebrew word *layla* is usually translated as "night" or "night time", which implies darkness, but the word used in Genesis 1:2 is *choshek*, which can also be translated as "destruction, misery, sorrow, or wickedness". So far Genesis 1:2 hints at something far deeper than just the earth being dark. Another verse that adds a strange spin on this concept is found in Isaiah, when referencing Lucifer's rebellion.

> "Yet thou shalt be brought down to hell, to the sides of the pit. They that see thee shall narrowly look upon thee, and consider thee, saying, Is this the man that made the earth to tremble, that did shake kingdoms; That made the world as a wilderness, and destroyed the cities thereof; that opened not the house of his prisoners? - Isaiah 14:15-17

Isaiah tells us that God did not create the earth *tohu* (void), but Genesis 1:2 tells us it became that way. Then there is Jeremiah's reference to "no man", but cities being destroyed out of God's anger. If we read the entire Bible we will never find a reference to all of the people being wiped out by God's anger. Even during the days of Noah, eight people survived the flood. When we get back to Isaiah, we also find him referencing the earth being turned into a wilderness, destroyed cities, and prisoners, all in reference to the fallen Lucifer. There seems to be more to the fall of Lucifer than the Sunday school version of events that we learn in church.

The Defiling of The Sanctuary

In this section we will use the Bible in an attempt to understand what may have happened during The Gap Theory. When

God is addressing the spiritual entity known as the King of Tyrus, in the book of Ezekiel, He reveals a very interesting aspect to where the physical part of the rebellion may have started.

> "Thou hast defiled thy sanctuaries by the multitude of thine iniquities, by the iniquity of thy traffic..." – Ezekiel 28:18

This first half of a verse is so profound that understanding it makes much of human history and the Bible make more sense. Lucifer's rebellion most likely began in one of the sanctuaries that he was in charge of during his service to God. It is unlikely that he would have continued serving in the sanctuary if he had already rebelled. The word for sanctuary in this verse is the Hebrew word *miqdash*. It refers to "a consecrated, sacred, or holy place." While the Bible speaks of the human body being the temple of the Holy Spirit, there is no such reference to the Holy Spirit indwelling angels, which leads us to the only alternative, and that is a physical temple.

The defiling of the Holy Place is a major part of human history. Pagan cultures would build temples for the purposes of human sacrifice and orgies dedicated to various gods and goddesses. While God required the blood of animals for forgiveness of sins, the gods and goddesses of the pagans required human blood to appease their wrath. God had very strict laws against homosexuality, bestiality, and incest, but it was widely practiced in pagan temples as a form of worship. The activities in the pagan temple seemed to be designed to directly conflict with the activities in the temple of God.

On the other hand we see the defiling of God's temple several times throughout history. One occasion was when Antiochus Epiphanes set up the statue of Zeus in the temple, slaughtered a pig on the altar, and completely defiled the temple. During the Olivet Discourse Jesus spoke of another temple defiling that will take place at the end of the age. In Matthew 24:15 Jesus refers to the "abomination of desolation spoken of by Daniel the prophet." Here is what Daniel says about the coming event:

> "And from the time that the daily sacrifice shall be taken away, and the abomination that maketh desolate set up,

> there shall be a thousand two hundred and ninety days." - Daniel 12:11

Daniel is clear on at least three occasions that the Abomination of Desolation is something that has to be set up. Most researchers agree that at some point the Antichrist will stand in the temple and declare himself to be above God and Christ. They base this conclusion on 2 Thessalonians 2:4. There is also another additional possibility that will happen in conjunction to him standing in the temple declaring himself to be God.

> "And he had power to give life unto the image of the beast, that the image of the beast should both speak, and cause that as many as would not worship the image of the beast should be killed." - Revelation 13:15

Notice that John does not call it a statue or idol, but uses the Greek word *eikon*, which means "a mirror like image", but what John is describing may not even be supernatural in nature.

Broadcasting The Abomination

We currently have two technologies that can project a mirror like image, and to someone in the past it would appear as if the image was given life. Those technologies are TV and hologram. John knew enough to know that he was not seeing the actual person of the Antichrist at the location, but something that looked like him in every way. How could John describe a TV or holographic image with the knowledge he had available to him at the time? Simply call it a living, mirror like image with the power to speak. If the Antichrist was watching from another location he could give the order to have people put to death for refusing to worship him. The image does not kill the people, but the image causes them to be killed. The above is just speculation, but Jesus makes a statement that seems a little farfetched unless you consider the possibility of our current level of technology as part of the prophecy.

> "When ye therefore shall see the abomination of desolation, spoken of by Daniel the prophet, stand in the holy place,

> (whoso readeth, let him understand:) Then let them which be in Judaea flee into the mountains: Let him which is on the housetop not come down to take anything out of his house: Neither let him which is in the field return back to take his clothes. " - Matthew 24:15-18

There is a very big problem with these verses if we were to take them at face value. The image is going to be inside of the temple and most likely inside the Holy of Holies, so how would someone on a roof or in the field see this event take place inside of a room that is inside of a building? Everything we know about physics tells us it is impossible to see through walls, meaning that there has to be a way for them to see it from these locations. As far as we know, this is the only period in history when people have possessed the capability of broadcasting an image that people can receive almost anywhere on the globe. Cell phones, PDAs, portable TV, etc. would allow someone in a field or on a roof top to see into the temple while the Abomination of Desolation is taking place. Keep in mind that God can see the end from the beginning, which means that neither Jesus nor Daniel were limited in their view of future events. The only limitations seemed to have been the language with which to describe these future events.

The person that commits what is known as the Abomination of Desolation is known as the Antichrist, but it is the origin of the Antichrist that is rarely, if ever touched on in the mainstream church; because it is even more controversial than many of the other subjects covered in this book.

The War of The God Men

There are at least two places in the Bible that speak of the *nackash* (serpent) having offspring. Both Genesis 3:15 and Isaiah 14:29 refer to the birth of Satan's son. We know that the serpent is Satan because of Revelation 12:9. There is nothing in either passage that indicates God was speaking in metaphors, similes, or any other parts of speech except literally. God had a Son so it is only logical that Satan would want to have his own son as well, in order to "be like the Most High". The rise of Sa-

Chapter 4: Rise of An Adversary

tan's son will lead to the ultimate battle, Christ vs. The Antichrist, the God-Man vs. The god-man.

If we look at the intention behind Satan having a son, we can see that it is probably one of the most sinister plots he has ever concocted since he rebelled against God. If there is any truth at all to the idea that Satan would have a son, we should see some clear similarities between his son and Christ. Let's compare Christ and the Antichrist and see just how intricate this plan to deceive mankind is.

1. **Hybrid Saviors:** In Genesis 3:15, God refers to the seed of the woman (Jesus) and the seed of the serpent (Antichrist). When Mary gave birth to Christ, He was part God and part Man (God-Man). Paul refers to Satan as "the god of this world" (2 Corinthians 4:4), which means the Antichrist will be part god and part man (god-man). While Jesus was the true savior, the Antichrist will present himself as the true savior of all mankind.

2. **Signs and Miracles:** While Christ walked the earth He healed the sick, gave sight to the blind, made the lame walk, and raised the dead. The Bible does not give us the details of what the Antichrist will do, but according to Matthew 24:24 the signs and wonders that would be displayed by the false Christs would be so powerful that it could potentially deceive the very elect.

3. **The Resurrection:** The resurrection of Christ is the foundation of Christianity. If He never got up there would be no reason for us to follow Him as the Messiah. In Revelation 13 we find one of the heads of the beast has been wounded to the point of death. Many people believe that this head represents the Antichrist. If that is true, Revelation 13:3 is clear that there will somehow be a supernatural resurrection of this head.

As we can see from the three examples above, even something simple as having a child becomes much more sinister and complex when in the hands of Satan. The arrival of the Antichrist is just one part of a much larger delusion.

> "And then shall that Wicked be revealed, whom the Lord shall consume with the spirit of his mouth, and shall destroy with the brightness of his coming: Even him, whose coming is after

> the working of Satan with all power and signs and lying wonders, And with all deceivableness of unrighteousness in them that perish; because they received not the love of the truth, that they might be saved. And for this cause God shall send them strong delusion, that they should believe a lie: That they all might be damned who believed not the truth, but had pleasure in unrighteousness." - 2 Thessalonians 2:8-12

I Will Be Like The Most High

Lucifer's ambition to be like the Most High may entail much more than just ruling over the angels and having a son. This was a very serious task that he was attempting to undertake, and assuming he was able to actually fight God, what did he plan to do with God if he won? Did he expect God to just take a back seat and allow him to reign? Did he think he could kill God? While Satan's defeat was inevitable, in his heart and mind he must have believed that he had a way to defeat God.

Opinion: I do not think that Satan fully understood what he was getting himself into. Part of his confidence may have come from his wisdom, beauty, and power, but the urge to be above God was a pride issue.

For those that have been conditioned their entire lives to believe that hybrids are the stuff that mythology is made of, the above information may not hold much weight, but it does not seem like these hybrids were being created for no reason. There actually seems to be a very valid reason for fallen angels, especially Lucifer, to attempt to create a hybrid creature.

Lucifer's ambition was to be like God in every way possible. In order to reach this goal, it was necessary for him to mimic what God had already created. The problem with hybrids is not that they appear all over the world in the myths and legends of other cultures, but that they appear in the Bible as guardians of God's throne. Is it possible that Satan was trying to copy creatures that were made by God?

> "Also out of the midst thereof came the likeness of four living creatures. And this was their appearance; they had the likeness of a man. And every one had four faces, and every one

> had four wings. And their feet were straight feet; and the sole of their feet was like the sole of a calf's foot: and they sparkled like the colour of burnished brass. And they had the hands of a man under their wings on their four sides; and they four had their faces and their wings. Their wings were joined one to another; they turned not when they went; they went every one straight forward. As for the likeness of their faces, they four had the face of a man, and the face of a lion, on the right side: and they four had the face of an ox on the left side; they four also had the face of an eagle." - Ezekiel 1:5-10

While it is not an exact description, the Assyrians worshiped a similar creature know as the *shedu*, and there are several similarities that stand out:

- Calf's Foot
- Multiple Wings
- Face of a Man

Is this a coincidence or is this proof that the hybrids of mythology have their origins in Lucifer's attempt to "be like the Most High?" This is where spiritual warfare crosses over into the physical realm. It is entirely possible that when we look at the carving of a Shedu, we are looking back into a period of history in which abominations conjured in the mind of Lucifer and the other fallen angels, actually walked the Earth. Even more disturbing is that science is actively pursuing the creation of animal/human hybrids much like those mentioned in the myths and legends all throughout history.

Is The Devil In Charge of Demons?

Sometimes we are guilty of accepting tradition as scripture and that can lead us into some very strange and non-Biblical beliefs that never get corrected. One traditionally held belief is that Satan is in charge of demons, but there are several reasons that he may not be in charge of these beings, so let's take a look at them.

In Genesis 6:4 the *b'nai ha Elohim* descended to earth because they lusted after human women, but there is not a single mention of Satan commanding them to do this. He may have been involved, but the Bible does not say that he was. It's possible that he used the event to his advantage in order to continue the corruption, but the original event may not have been his idea. According to Genesis, the *nephilim* eventually died and many of us believe their disembodied spirits may have become what we refer to as demons. Many Christians equate Beelzebub, Lord of the Flies, with Satan and if that is true, the Pharisees' words to Jesus are very important.

> "But when the Pharisees heard it, they said, This fellow doth not cast out devils, but by Beelzebub the prince of the devils." - Matthew 12:24

Opinion: I do not believe that any words are in the Bible by accident. Every word seems to have an intended purpose, and in order to really understand what is being said, we need to consider exactly what is being said.

The Greek word used in Matthew 12:24 is *archon*, which means chief or ruler, but we will come back to the word *archon* in a moment. In Revelation 9:11 we discover that Apollyon is referred to as the king of the locusts from the Abyss. Traditional teaching says that these locusts are really demons, so our next step is to look at the Greek word for king.

- *Basileus* - king, king of kings

Think of the above words in terms of military rank. A five star general would be an *archon* but the President would be the *basileus*. Here is where we step into an interesting problem. Many people think that Apollyon and Satan are one in the same simply because Apollyon means "destroyer". If this is true it presents several problems to traditional interpretation:

1. **Possibility:** Beelzebub and Appolyon are two different angels with two different ranks.
2. **Possibility:** Beelzebub and Appolyon are the same angel with contradicting rank descriptions.
3. **Possibility:** Traditional interpretations of Beelzebub and Appolyon as Satan are wrong.

Chapter 4: Rise of An Adversary

According to Revelation 9, an angel comes from heaven with the key to the bottomless pit and releases a horde of evil locust like creatures. Apollyon is referred to as the angel of the bottomless pit, but this is never a description applied to Satan. In fact, Satan is only bound and sent to the bottomless pit after these creatures are released. There are only two possibilities for the origin of Apollyon and both of them exclude him from being Satan.

1. **Possibility:** Apollyon is the angel that comes from heaven with the key.
2. **Possibility:** The angel with the key releases Apollyon from the bottomless pit.

The same angel with the key returns in Revelation 20, binds Satan, and casts him into the bottomless pit, which automatically disqualifies this angel from being Satan in Revelation 9, if he is indeed Apollyon. If Apollyon came from the pit, he cannot be Satan because Satan is not bound in the pit until the 1,000 year reign of Christ. The ultimate conclusion is that Satan is either Beelzebub or Apollyon, or neither of the two because context shows us that he cannot be both. If the locusts in Revelation 9 are indeed demons, it means that Satan is not in charge of the demons. This is just one reason why we really need to examine the traditional teaching on just about everything we read in the Bible. Given enough time, people will begin to believe and repeat tradition without question, even if it makes no sense at all, and in some cases even contradicts the actual words of the Bible.

The Satanic Plot

The entire Bible is filled with sort of a back and forth between God and Lucifer. This futile battle of the minds comes as a result of God's declaration in Genesis 3:15 that the Seed of the woman would eventually lead to Lucifer's destruction. Lucifer is constantly trying to outsmart God, only to be one upped at every turn. As we turn the pages of the Bible, we can actually chart the strategy in every book of the Bible. Here are just a few of the major satanic attempts to stop the Seed of the woman from destroying him:

- Cain kills Abel (Genesis 4:8)
- 1st Nephilim outbreak (Genesis 6)
- 2nd Nephilim outbreak near Sodom (Genesis 14)
- 1st Holocaust by Pharaoh (Exodus 1:22)
- 3rd Nephilim outbreak - Promised Land (Numbers 13:33)
- Failed Holocaust by Haman (Esther 3:9)
- 2nd Holocaust of the Jewish children (Matthew 2)
- The temptation of Christ (Mark 1:13)
- The betrayal of Christ by Judas (Luke 22:3)
- 3rd Holocaust by Hitler (January 30, 1933 – May 8, 1945)
- The Six Days War (June 6, 1967)
- Current situation surrounding Israel
- 4th Holocaust to come (Matthew 24:15-21, Revelation 12:12-13)

Most recently, a false and deceptive doctrine known as Serpent Seed Theology has once again found its way into mainstream churches, and it's entire focus is on hatred for the real Jews, while at the same time claiming that Serpent Seed Theology believers are the real Jews. The Bible refers to this false claim as blasphemy.

> "I know thy works, and tribulation, and poverty, (but thou art rich) and I know the blasphemy of them which say they are Jews, and are not, but are the synagogue of Satan." - Revelation 2:9

There is a reason that Lucifer is focusing his efforts on God's chosen people, the Jewish nation. At first it was to stop the Seed of the woman from being born based on the prophecy in Genesis 3:15, but after the failure of that plan, the focus has changed to wiping out the Jewish nation completely in an attempt to avoid the 144,000 in Revelation Chapter 7. If Satan can successfully wipe out God's people, he will have proved to the world that God is not in complete control and it will give him hope that he can stop his eventual destiny in the Lake of Fire. However, he has not and will not be successful in his attempts.

Another possibility as to why the angels would have attempted to destroy mankind multiple times is out of desperation. The first group of Watchers may have been bound and

Chapter 4: Rise of An Adversary

delivered into outer darkness, but that does not mean that more angels would not or could not attempt to use this strategy again. As a society we know that if we murder someone, chances are we will be caught and end up in prison, but that does not stop people from committing murder on a daily basis. It is possible that these angels were simply doing everything in their power to stop their coming judgment. There are some that assume that no other angels would attempt to mix with mankind because of the punishment delivered on the first set of angels that made this attempt. The fallen angels have already been sentenced to an eternity in the Lake of Fire, so there is no reason to believe that they would be scared of "angelic prison" (outer darkness). Both scripture and history seem to disagree with those that hold this view. Angels in general seem to be completely misunderstood because the Bible is rarely used when developing theories about what angels are and what they can do.

How Powerful Is Satan?

Many people seem to have the common misconception that Satan can just be easily defeated through songs and a few words. In fact, there are a lot of non-Biblical ideas that float around Christian circles concerning Satan. Here are just a few:

1. Satan cannot stand in the presence of praise.
2. Satan cannot read the Bible.
3. Satan cannot enter a church building.

All of these beliefs sound good and may sound comforting to believers, but they are all 100% false and based on nothing more than superstitious tradition, and according to the context of Mark 7, it is the traditions of men that make void the word of God. Let's address the above three problems using nothing more than scripture and a little bit of discernment.

1. Many Christians believe that Satan was once in charge of heavenly praise based on Ezekiel 28:13. There is nothing in the Bible that indicates that Satan can no longer stand in the presence of praise. This is tradition and not scripture.

2. The myth that Satan cannot read the Bible is a direct contradiction of the Bible. In fact, there are two occasions in which Satan attempts to twist God's word for his own purposes. Once is in Genesis 3, where Satan attempts to twist that words that God spoke to Adam and Eve. The second time was while he was tempting Jesus and he quoted Psalm 91 almost word for word.

3. The belief that Satan cannot stand on holy ground was probably made popular by Hollywood movies. In fact, in the Bible we find the exact opposite. In Job 1 and 2, Satan walks right up to God with the other angels and they have a conversation concerning Job. If Satan can stand in the presence of God, what would stop him from entering a church building?

Satan is not to be worshipped, but he is also not to be taken lightly as if he is just some cartoonish adversary of God. This is the same being that had the audacity to start a war with God and attempt to thwart Christ by using the very scriptures that prophesied His coming. According to Ezekiel 28:3 he is "wiser than Daniel." According to 1 Peter 5:8 he walks around like a roaring lion seeking whom he may devour. The weak and cowardly do not go looking for trouble. Also make note that Peter specifically said that he is looking for whom he may devour. In order for a lion to devour it's pray, it must first gain victory over its intended victim. Satan is not playing games, he is playing for keeps.

> "Yet Michael the archangel, when contending with the devil he disputed about the body of Moses, durst not bring against him a railing accusation, but said, The Lord rebuke thee." - Jude 1:9

In other words, Michael did not get himself hyped up by singing songs and he did not defeat Satan by calling him "a lie" or any of the other traditional things that Christians say that hype themselves into thinking they can take on Satan in a one on one fight. What many people do not understand about what was going on between Michael and Satan is that it was not a physical confrontation, it was just a *diakrinomenos dielegeto* (Greek), which means, "a back and forth argument or discussion."

Chapter 4: Rise of An Adversary

If we continue digging into the Greek, we discover something else odd about this entire scenario. According to Jude, Michael "durst (dared) not bring against him a railing accusation." The Greek word for durst (dared) is *tolmao* which means, "to be bold or have courage." The phrase "railing accusation" is the Greek phrase *blasphemia krisis*, which means, "abusive language". To put this in perspective, Michael is one of the Chief Princes according to Daniel 10:13, he will fight with Satan during the end times according to Revelation 12, and even he knew enough to watch his mouth when simply arguing with Satan. Michael is no coward, but he is also not stupid. Satan is very powerful, which is why Michael said, "the Lord rebuke thee". Contrary to tradition, to rebuke something does not mean it has to leave you alone. The meaning of *epitimao* (rebuke) means, "to give a warning to prevent something from going wrong or escalating." Michael used a threat directly from God when he said, "the Lord rebuke thee." In other words, "leave it alone before it gets out of hand." A rebuke, based on context is a threat or a promise of confrontation if the current situation does not change. It is a declaration of spiritual warfare.

Satan was not and is not afraid of Michael or any of the other angels, but he does take the Lord seriously. We as Christians need to recognize that there is an enemy roaming free that not even one of the most powerful angels in God's command will get disrespectful with in a conversation, and we should also conduct ourselves accordingly when we make the decisions to sing certain songs and make certain statements about Satan. With the exception of an outright physical confrontation between all of heaven, using a rebuke from the Lord is the only way that scripture gives us to deal with Satan.

The Breakdown

As Christians we need to be very aware of who our adversary is and what he is all about. He is not some comical character with red tights, horns, and a pitchfork running around hell. He is God's former highest ranking angel and he is probably more powerful than we can imagine. Even though he is powerful, he is still a created being and not worthy of worship. His power is to be respected but never worshiped. He is by no means equal in power or intelligence to God and he is fighting a losing battle. However, failure to recognize that there is indeed a real enemy can lead us to become casualties of war. Satan is referred to as the "god of this world" and we need to keep that in mind when it comes to politics and current events. Every event is not a sign of the end of the age, but rarely are political events without some spiritual influence.

Chapter in Review

- What is the Devil?
- What are the names of our enemy?
- How many "I Wills" were there?
- Is Satan in charge of demons?
- What are some traditional myths about Satan?
- Should Satan ever be worshiped?

Critical Thinking

- What can't the Devil do?
- Did the rebellion start in heaven?
- How far did Satan go in an attempt to be like God?
- How powerful is Satan?

The Plan of Salvation

The plan of salvation is not difficult or complicated at all. In fact it can be summed up in one single verse. All you need to do in order to be saved is the following:

> That if thou shalt confess with thy mouth the Lord Jesus, and shalt believe in thine heart that God hath raised him from the dead, thou shalt be saved." - Romans 10:9

If you have accepted Christ, your next step should be to get your hands on a King James Version of the Bible. Before joining any church, you should have a good foundation in scripture

Chapter 4: Rise of An Adversary

without the influences of any teacher. Once you have a general understanding of scripture, visit a few churches before deciding on a church home. Make sure you check behind the pastor and do not just accept their word for anything without checking (Acts 17:11). If asking questions is discouraged, steer clear of that church at all costs.

Key Scriptures For Review

- Genesis 2
- Genesis 3
- Psalm 91
- Psalms 104
- Isaiah 4
- Isaiah 14
- Isaiah 45
- Jeremiah 4
- Ezekiel 1
- Ezekiel 28
- Daniel 12
- Matthew 12
- Matthew 4
- Matthew 24
- 2 Corinthians 11
- Galatians 1
- 2 Thessalonians 2
- Jude 1
- Revelation 2
- Revelation 12
- Revelation 13

Submit Your Questions

If you have more questions about spiritual warfare, angels, demons, the supernatural, or the Bible in general, you are welcome to submit your questions to me personally. Answers to your questions will be posted as an article on the website for everyone to see.

www.MinisterFortson.com

Chapter 5: The War in Heaven

> The direct use of force is such a poor solution to any problem, it is generally employed only by small children and large nations. - David Friedman

The war in heaven is a foundational turning point in scripture. Aside from the Resurrection of Christ it is possibly the most important event in history. This event is so important because it is the enemy's official attempt at taking the throne of God. It also completely changes the direction of all creation. In the last chapter we learned about the angel that rose to lead this rebellion, but was the fight for heaven an actual event or just an imaginary tale from writers with an overactive imagination? On TV, almost every day, we can turn on the news and see the devastation of warfare, poverty, and sin in the world. Just imagine what would happen if God and His angels went to war with very powerful angels that are opposed to Him. The outcome would be devastating. In this chapter we are going to explore this war and the resulting consequences on all of creation.

The Timeframe of The War

Many cultures believe that the battle for heaven may have spilled over into the earth realm. If this is true, it may account for some very strange passages in the Bible. In Genesis 1:2, the English version says, "the earth was without form and void." However, there are some that believe the word "was" is a mistranslation. The Hebrew word used is *hayah*, which means "to become" or "became". *Hayah* is the same word translated as "became" in Genesis 19:26 in reference to Lot's wife. The phrase "without form and void", are the words *tohu vavohu* in Hebrew. *Tohu* means "confused" or "ruined". Vavohu means "desolate" or "destroyed". The meanings of these words lead some to believe that this is the timeframe in which the war in heaven occurred and as a result left the earth in ruins.

This period of time occurs after the creation of earth, but before the creation of mankind. If this concept sounds new, it is probably because of the way Genesis 1 has traditionally been taught. Genesis 1:1 tells us, "in the beginning God created the heaven and the earth." Because of the words in Genesis 1:2, there are some that believe that the rest of Genesis 1 is a restoration and not the original creation. As we will see over and over again, this concept is present in other cultures as well. The Bible is only one of many ancient texts to hint at some major supernatural rebellion the occurred after the creation of earth, but before the creation of mankind.

Disclaimer: The following references from other cultures are not meant to validate their exact version of events, but to support the belief that there was indeed a war for heaven at some point in history. One common theme that we will see among all of these stories is that even though the original battle is for control of heaven, the beings that claimed to be the victors are always confined to the realms of the earth and Underworld.

The War According To The Sumerians

According to Sumerian legend, there were two groups that went to war for the heavenly realm. These two groups were the *Igigi* and the *Anunnaki*. According to the story, the *Anunnaki* needed a leader, and Marduk, represented by the serpent and dragon, stepped up. The story also goes on to say that the *Anunnaki* won the war, but came to earth and became the gods of the earth and underworld. The Sumerians viewed the Anunnaki as oppressive to mankind. On the other hand, the *Igigi* were considered to be the guardians of the heavenly realm.

The War According To The Norse

The Norse refer to this war for the heavens as the *Aesir - Vanir* War. According to the Norse, this war took place between two sets of gods, and the two groups eventually come to coexist as one group. Although they all merge as a single group, there are still gods that are completely evil and gods that are completely good. In most cases these evil gods still have access to heaven, but no longer reside there. This may be similar to the story that we find in Job 1 and 2, when the sons of God come to present themselves to the Lord.

The War According To The Greeks

Hesiod's believed in the Golden Age of mankind. This was the period in which a race of beings similar to modern man were created, but were more angelic than human. During this same time frame, it is believed that there was a major war that lasted for ten years, known as the *Titanomachy*. This war was believed to be between the Titans and the Olympians. It is at this point that Zeus and the Olympians rise to power and assume control by banishing the titans to *tartarus*. Tartarus is the same word translated as "hell" in 2 Peter 2:4.

The Ties That Bind

It is important to completely keep everything in context when dealing with the "mythology" of other cultures. Even though the above stories contain different names, the motive and events are still the same. Two groups of gods want control of the heavenly realm. The war usually begins with one group rebelling against the powers that be, and the other group defending heaven. Another common element to the stories is the final outcome. In the Bible, the fallen angels that are cast from heaven begin to deceive mankind. In the Sumerian legends, the Anunnaki are said to have won the war, but end up bound to the earth and underworld, and begin to oppress mankind. In the Greek legend, Zeus and the Olympians are said to have won the war, but end up bound to the earth and underworld, and become the tormentors of mankind. Based on the similarities of the stories, there are only two possible conclusions:

1. All of these stories copied a common source.
2. These stories stem from very real events that were preserved through legend over the course of history.

As we will see later, the latter is a more likely scenario. As a result of war, there is always the following aftermath that results.

The Aftermath of War

Job 38:7 tells us that "the sons of God" shouted for joy when the earth was created, so we know that angels were created sometime prior to Genesis 1:1. What happened between Genesis 1:1-2 that caused the earth to become confused and destroyed? 1 Corinthians 14:33 tells us that God is not the author of confusion, so something or someone else seems to have caused the earth to becoming confused (*tohu*).

> "For thus saith the LORD that created the heavens; God himself that formed the earth and made it; he hath established it, **he created it not in vain**, he formed it to be inhabited: I am the LORD; and there is none else." - Isaiah 45:18

Here we see that God did not create the earth in "vain". The word translated as vain is the Hebrew word *tohu*. Genesis 1:2 says the earth was *tohu*, which is the same word used in Isaiah 45:18. Paul tells us that God is not the author of confusion and Isaiah tells us that God did not create the earth confused. Are there any clues in the Bible that reveal to us how the earth got that way? T

> "I beheld the earth, and, lo, it was without form, and void; and the heavens, and they had no light. I beheld the mountains, and, lo, they trembled, and all the hills moved lightly. I beheld, and, lo, **there was no man**, and all the birds of the heavens were fled. I beheld, and, lo, the fruitful place was a wilderness, and all the cities thereof were broken down at the presence of the LORD, and by his fierce anger." - Jeremiah 4:23-26

Here Jeremiah is viewing the earth as we see in Genesis 1:1 (without form and void), but he adds a few interesting observations.

- The mountains trembled.
- There was no man.
- The birds have fled.
- The fruitful place has become a wilderness.
- The cities were destroyed.
- God is angry.

Chapter 5: The War In Heaven

In order to put together the pieces, we first need to ask ourselves if this is consistent with the Genesis account. According to the last part of Genesis 1:2, "darkness" was upon the face of the deep. The Hebrew word *layla* is usually translated as "night" or "night time", which implies darkness. However, the word used instead of *layla* in Genesis 1:2 is *choshek*, which can also be translated as "destruction, misery, sorrow, or wickedness". The choice of wording here seems to indicate something far deeper than just the earth being dark. Even though this is interesting, we need to find a Biblical connection between Satan and him turning the world into a wilderness.

> "How art thou fallen from heaven, O Lucifer, son of the morning! how art thou cut down to the ground, which didst weaken the nations! For thou hast said in thine heart, I will ascend into heaven, I will exalt my throne above the stars of God: I will sit also upon the mount of the congregation, in the sides of the north: I will ascend above the heights of the clouds; I will be like the most High. Yet thou shalt be brought down to hell, to the sides of the pit. They that see thee shall narrowly look upon thee, and consider thee, saying, Is this the man that made the earth to tremble, that did shake kingdoms; **That made the world as a wilderness,** and destroyed the cities thereof; that opened not the house of his prisoners?
> - Isaiah 14:13-17

Lucifer's rebellion originally starts in his heart and eventually manifests as an all out war on God and His creation. Upon Lucifer's final defeat, people recognize him as the one that made the earth to tremble, shook kingdoms, and turned the world into a wilderness. This seems to be very consistent with what Jeremiah saw and what Genesis 1:2 says in Hebrew. This war was devastating and possibly plunged the entire universe into darkness, which explains why God's first restorative act was to bring light into existence.

Theory: The angels may have had a civilization on earth that was created after Genesis 1:1, but was destroyed before Genesis 1:2, because of Lucifer's rebellion. This civilization may have had Lucifer as its leader, which may explain the events in the garden, after Adam was given dominion over the earth.

Much of the restoration/re-creation after this resulting war is covered in my book, <u>As The Days of Noah Were</u>, therefore we are going to focus on the rest of the battle that has been raging since the creation of mankind.

The War Spills Over

When we get to Genesis 3, Satan is already an enemy of God and mankind. My book, Religion and Relationship, details the father/son relationship between God and Lucifer. Even after leading the rebellion for heaven and possibly destroying the earth, Satan is not sentenced to death or the Lake of Fire. It is not until Satan extends his war to include mankind that God declares the following:

> "And I will put enmity between thee and the woman, and between thy seed and her seed; it shall bruise thy head, and thou shalt bruise his heel." - Genesis 3:15

Here is where the war takes a turn for the worse. Satan has effectively led Adam and Eve in rebellion/disobedience against God, and he knew the prophecy that they would die the day that they ate the fruit of the Tree of Knowledge of Good and Evil, but what he did not count on was it being a day in God's time frame (1,000 years). It is possible that Satan thought he had just ended God's new creation, only to find out that was not the case.

Once God addressed the situation, He added insult to injury. Not only had Satan's plan failed in immediate result, his punishment is to be destroyed by a human child. As we will see, humans were created below the angels, but will eventually be given authority to judge the angels. Imagine being a prideful angel with hopes to ascend to the throne of God, and then being told you would be destroyed by a part of creation lower than yourself. It is the ultimate insult. Satan, being who he is, cannot sit back and just allow this happen. The only option is to wipe out the human race and attempt to stop his coming destruction.

Chapter 5: The War In Heaven

The Final Solution

Please take a second to read the quote at the beginning of this chapter again. Satan did not know this information at the time, and according to the Bible, he was the first being in the universe to use force in an attempt to get what he wanted. That attempt was an epic fail, and according to the Bible, Satan is wiser than Daniel (Ezekiel 28:3). There is no doubt that Satan learned from his first mistake and would not risk another direct attack against God or his creation, unless it was an act of desperation.

Disclaimer: The following is nothing more than my opinion based solely on the pattern of events presented in the Bible. I invite and encourage you to follow Acts 17:11 and check all of the references for yourself.

History testifies that the best way to wipe out an enemy is not through direct physical confrontation, but through biological warfare. Using diseases or poisons that can be ingested or contracted and then spread to other humans is more effective than shooting them one by one. Anthrax is a perfect example of this concept. In Genesis 6, we find this strategy being used by the "sons of God". Their mixing with the "daughters of men" caused unnatural hybrid offspring to be born, and these stories are reflected in every culture on earth. This was a genetic assault on the human race, and as a result, God completely destroys everything except for eight people and a small number of animals. What we are going to focus on now are the post flood occurrences of *nephilim*/giants and how God dealt with the genetic contamination and kept it from getting out of control.

Zombie Apocalypse

According to Genesis 6:12, all flesh had become corrupted, and in order to avoid the same situation after the flood, God becomes proactive and wipes out almost all genetically tainted tribes. One of the tribes that were notorious for producing hybrids was known as the *Rephaim*. The name *Rephaim* in Hebrew means (ghosts/dead ones/shades), yet they were very much alive. What we literally have are "the living dead". To make this situation even stranger than it is, the prophet Isaiah tells us that the *Rephaim* will have no resurrection at all. The following is from the Young's Literal Translation of Isaiah 26:14:

> "Dead -- they live not, Rephaim, they rise not, Therefore Thou hast inspected and dost destroy them, Yea, thou destroyest all their memory." - Young's Literal Translation

If we check this verse in the KJV, the word *Rephaim* is simply translated as "dead". To put the entire statement in perspective, Isaiah is talking about the resurrection of mankind; he then specifically refers to the *Rephaim* not rising from the dead. According to Jewish legend, the *Rephaim* were an entire tribe of blood drinking, flesh eating, angel/human hybrids that terrorized mankind. The actions of the *Rephaim* may also be the origin of the myriad stories about giants that devoured human flesh and drank blood. The *Rephaim* would also take human wives, have offspring, which in turn did the same, thus passing along their DNA for multiple generations.

These giants first appear in Genesis 14, which was less than 400 years after Noah's flood. At the same time The War of The Five Kings erupts and Chedorlaomer begins to slaughter the *Rephaim*, and during this slaughter, the kings of Sodom and Gomorrah come to their aid. This is the first and only connection we see between Sodom, Gomorrah, and the *Rephaim*. Several chapters later, we find two angels making a personal visit to Sodom in order to see if it was really as bad as God had heard it was. Once inside the city, the men of Sodom attempt to physically rape the angels. Here is where we encounter the traditions of men once again. In some churches it is taught that it would have been impossible for the men of the city to rape the angels, but there are several elements of the story that seem to prove the exact opposite:

- Lot puts himself in danger to protect the angels.
- Lot offers his daughters to the mob.
- The angels blind the men so they can get Lot out of the city.
- They shut the door to keep the blind men out.

Chapter 5: The War In Heaven

There seemed to be a very real danger and very real possibility that these men could accomplish their goal of raping the angels if they had not been blinded. This attempted sexual assault was the final straw, and as soon as Lot and his family are safely placed outside of the city, the angels destroyed four of the five cities on the plain (Luke 17:29). God's original intent was to destroy all five cities, but Lot negotiated with the angels to spare Zoar so that he and his family can escape there.

All five of these cities had already aligned themselves with several hybrid tribes, and then there was the attempted rape of the angels. It is very likely that many of the *Rephaim*, *Emim*, and several other *nephilim* tribes decreased greatly in number when these cities on the plain were destroyed. The first time these hybrids appeared on earth, God destroyed it with a flood. Then we see them align with Sodom, Gomorrah, and three other cities, and the result is God completely obliterating four of the five cities.

> "And as it was in the days of Noe, so shall it be also in the days of the Son of man. They did eat, they drank, they married wives, they were given in marriage, until the day that Noah entered into the ark, and the flood came, and destroyed them all. Likewise also as it was in the days of Lot; they did eat, they drank, they bought, they sold, they planted, they builded; But the same day that Lot went out of Sodom it rained fire and brimstone from heaven, and destroyed them all." - Luke 17:26-29

Jesus compares the end of the world with both the days of Noah and the days of Lot. According to both scripture and many beliefs surrounding these events, they have several things in common:

- Wickedness of mankind become a problem.
- Hybrid creatures live among mankind.
  Humans and angels become sexually active with each other.
- God destroys all but a few that are saved by grace.

After Sodom and the rest of the cities are destroyed, the flesh eating, blood drinking, living dead, known as the *Rephaim* emerge again. Much of the *Rephaim* activity is hard to trace in the King James Bible because it is translated as "giant" in most places, but thankfully, the New International Version's conservative, anti-supernatural position, leaves the word completely un-translated, and as a result, makes it much easier to trace.

According to the Bible, there were a very small number of the *Rephaim* that survived the destruction on the plain. In fact, after the destruction of the cities, the *Rephaim* are not mentioned again until we reach the days of David, where there are only six of them. Five of them are named and one is un-named. These names are listed in my book, <u>As The Days of Noah Were</u>. The following verses in the NIV leave the word *Rapha* (giant), the singular of the word *Rephaim*, un-translated because of its anti-supernatural position.

- 2 Samuel 21:16
- 2 Samuel 21:18
- 2 Samuel 21:20
- 2 Samuel 21:22
- 1 Chronicles 4:12
- 1 Chronicles 8:2
- 1 Chronicles 20:6
- 1 Chronicles 20:8

> "And Ishbibenob, which was of the sons of the giant, the weight of whose spear weighed three hundred shekels of brass in weight, he being girded with a new sword, thought to have slain David. But Abishai the son of Zeruiah succoured him, and smote the Philistine, and killed him. Then the men of David sware unto him, saying, Thou shalt go no more out with us to battle, that thou quench not the light of Israel." - 2 Samuel 21:16-17

In the above verses, the word giant is the Hebrew word *Rapha*, from which the *Rephaim* descend. Here we see that David was rescued from being killed by one of these hybrid giants. As time passes, eventually David's men kill the remaining *Rephaim*. The events on the plain and the events in David's time are just two examples of spiritual warfare being Beyond Flesh and Blood. The tainted DNA from these hybrids was passed on to their offspring and according to many legends, they were sexually active with animals too. God had zero tolerance for this and as a result issues seemingly harsh commands concerning several groups of people in the Bible:

> Now go and smite Amalek, and utterly destroy all that they have, and spare them not; but slay both man and woman, infant and suckling, ox and sheep, camel and ass." – 1 Samuel 15:3

Everything touched by these hybrid abominations had to be wiped out, including the children and animals. God takes the destruction of the hybrids very seriously to the point that two leaders of Israel were punished for not obeying his commands. Saul actually attempts to keep the hybrid king Agag alive, and as a result God strips him of his rights to the throne of Israel (1 Samuel 15:26). The other leader that was removed and not allowed to finish the journey that he started was Moses, partially because of the following event concerning the hybrids:

> "And there we saw the giants, the sons of Anak, which come of the giants: and we were in our own sight as grasshoppers, and so we were in their sight." – Numbers 13:33

This single report from the ten spies about Nephilim in the Promised Land causes Moses and all of the children of Israel to be afraid. As a result, Moses did not invade the Promised Land as he was supposed to do. These giants were not just normal men with a height issue. There was something genetically different about these supernatural/natural hybrids, but what was it?

Supernatural Biological Warfare

To many people the belief in literal giants and hybrids sounds like the stuff of mythology so they completely disregard it without doing any further research into the matter. Proverbs 13:18 says that it is foolish to answer a matter before hearing it, so it is important that we investigate every claim after hearing it (Acts 17:11). If the concept of tainted DNA and strange genetics has any truth to it, there should be some indication of it in the Bible. As we progress through the book, we will see many indications that something out of the ordinary was and is going on, concerning human DNA.

The Breakdown

The angelic rebellion against the Creator is not just a quaint story reflected in almost every culture on earth by coincidence. The war in heaven was a very real event that is still continuing around us every second of every day, and will continue until the return of Christ. Once we understand this, the goals of science and politics soon begin to make sense. Ultimately it does not come down to whether you are Democrat or Republican, but whether or not you are choosing God or the Devil. Divisive issues such as political parties have a tendency to keep our eyes off of what is really going on, which is a Satanic charade that will ultimately end in a war between, Satan, humanity, and Christ.

Chapter In Review

- When did the war in heaven happen?
- What does the Biblical version of the war in heaven have in common with other cultures?
- What happened to the fallen angels after the war was over?
- Has the war in heaven affected mankind?
- Was there a Satanic plot to tamper with human DNA?

Critical Thinking

- Was the war in heaven real?
- Why is the war in heaven important?
- Do the mythologies from other cultures have any truth to them?
- Are fallen angels still at war with God?
- Are fallen angels at war with humans?
- Should we be worried about scientific interest in human DNA?

Chapter 5: The War In Heaven

The Plan of Salvation

The plan of salvation is not difficult or complicated at all. In fact it can be summed up in one single verse. All you need to do in order to be saved is the following:

> That if thou shalt confess with thy mouth the Lord Jesus, and shalt believe in thine heart that God hath raised him from the dead, thou shalt be saved." - Romans 10:9

If you have accepted Christ, your next step should be to get your hands on a King James Version of the Bible. Before joining any church, you should have a good foundation in scripture without the influences of any teacher. Once you have a general understanding of scripture, visit a few churches before deciding on a church home. Make sure you check behind the pastor and do not just accept their word for anything without checking (Acts 17:11). If asking questions is discouraged, steer clear of that church at all costs.

Key Scriptures For Review

- Genesis 3
- Genesis 19
- Numbers 13
- 1 Samuel 15
- Isaiah 14
- Isaiah 26
- Isaiah 45
- Jeremiah 4
- Luke 17

Submit Your Questions

If you have more questions about spiritual warfare, angels, demons, the supernatural, or the Bible in general, you are welcome to submit your questions to me personally. Answers to your questions will be posted as an article on the website for everyone to see.

www.MinisterFortson.com

Chapter 6: The Abilities of Angels

"Every general knows that the first rule of warfare is, 'Know your enemy' And knowing your enemy demands that you name your enemy." - Chuck Colson

When we consider that beings handmade by God decided to form a rebellion, it should make us stop and consider just how powerful these beings are. What was it that made 1/3 of the angels attempt to overthrow the God of all creation? We have all probably heard the saying, "with great power comes great responsibility", so in this chapter, we are going to explore twenty one different abilities of angels, according to the Bible.

A Misunderstanding of Angels

Much of the information that we have about angels is based on Church tradition that has been modified over hundreds of years. As we read through the Bible, we find that many of these traditions do not actually appear in scripture. For example, Cherubim are not winged babies, angels do not have halos, and no male angels are depicted as having only two wings.

Imagery like the picture above is partly responsible for the commercialized and cartoonish depiction of angels. According to the Bible and many outside sources, angels are not only messengers of God, but fierce warriors that are able to stand in His presence. They are also capable of things which defy much of what we refer to as reality.

Angels Deliver Messages To The Living.

Many people believe that being a messenger is the only function of an angel, but it is just the first of many. All through the Bible we see angels delivering messages to various people for different reasons. The following scriptures in the Bible depict angels delivering messages from God to mankind.

- Sodom and Gomorrah (Genesis 19:15)
- The birth of John the Baptist (Luke 1:13)
- The Birth of Jesus (Luke 2:21)

The Bible is not the only text that depicts supernatural messengers that travel between the spiritual and physical realms. Perhaps one of the most famous of these extra Biblical messengers is the Greek god Hermes.

Chapter 6: The Abilities of Angels

Although Hermes is possibly the most famous, other cultures wrote of beings that were messengers very similar to the angels:

- Egypt: Anubis
- Rome: Mercury
- Indonesia: Raja Indainda
- Etruscan: Turms
- Hindu: Agni
- Akkadian: Papsukkal
- Chile: Grandpa Wenteyao
- Mesopotamia: Zaqar

As we can clearly see, the concept of supernatural messengers is present in many different cultures. It is possible that it was not just the Hebrews that encountered angels, but in reality, many cultures had these encounters. However, their interpretation of what these angels were may have differed depending on the culture. This explanation may help us shed light on the beings the pagans referred to as the gods.

Angels Can Appear and Disappear

Angels seem to possess the ability to appear and disappear at will. A more accurate description of their power would be the ability to allow us to see them or not. One clear example we find is Numbers 22:31 where Balaam encounters an angel that will not let him pass. The donkey sees the angel, but Balaam does not until the angel allows his eyes to be opened. There are several other places in scripture where this appearing and disappearing act occurs:

- Judges 6:21
- Luke 22:43
- Acts 12:10

Once again, we find a valid explanation of why people claimed to have encountered gods or other beings with the ability to appear and disappear at will. Church tradition teaches that the fallen angels were stripped of these powers, however, there is no such story in the Bible, and no other culture makes mention of those beings that they consider evil, being stripped of their powers. It is likely that both the good and bad angels maintained their ability. This ability may also be responsible for many of the apparitions people experience during a haunting. Humans have a tendency to believe what they see instead of using spiritual discernment when it comes to the sudden appearance of a dead friend or family member. This is a touchy subject for many people because they would like to believe that the dead are contacting them from the afterlife. While it is possible, but not likely that a dead loved one is making contact from beyond the grave, chances are it is a fallen angel attempting to draw in an unsuspecting victim.

Angels Can Change Form

The ability to change form seems like something out of a sci-fi movie. In fact, most sci-fi movies refer to this ability as "shapeshifting." The Bible makes mention of one specific fallen angel with the ability to appear as something that he is not.

> "And no marvel; for Satan himself is transformed into an angel of light." - 2 Corinthians 11:14

For those that think the above verse is just a figure of speech, the Greek word for transform reveals it to be much more than that. The Greek word used is *metaschematizo*, which means, "to change the outward appearance, to transform". If Satan has the power to transform his outer appearance into that of an angel of light, it means that he is not an angel of light. It is also possible that he is not the only angel capable of making this transformation. Here are several more verses from the Bible that demonstrate the angelic ability to shapeshift:

- Genesis 3
- Exodus 3:2
- Exodus 14:19
- Judges 13:6
- Hebrews 13:2
- Jude 1:6

Chapter 6: The Abilities of Angels

Perhaps the most interesting of these Biblical references comes from Jude 1:6. Again, we turn to the pages of the Bible for a very straight forward statement concerning them changing their form:

> "And the angels which kept not their first estate, but left their own habitation, he hath reserved in everlasting chains under darkness unto the judgment of the great day." – Jude 1:6

The English version, sounds like these angels simply left their position of power or their heavenly home. Someone reading this could conclude that this leaving of their habitation was a result of Lucifer's rebellion, but the Greek puts a slightly different spin on it. The word translated as habitation is the Greek word *oiketerion*, and as we will see, it specifically refers to a spiritual body. Paul also uses the same word in 2 Corinthians. Much to the dismay of those that do not believe what the scripture says about the angels, the word *oiketerion* is only used two times in all of scripture, and both times it refers to a spiritual body.

> "For we know that if our earthly house of this tabernacle were dissolved, we have a building of God, an house not made with hands, eternal in the heavens. For in this we groan, earnestly desiring to be clothed upon with our house which is from heaven: If so be that being clothed we shall not be found naked. For we that are in this tabernacle do groan, being burdened: not for that we would be unclothed, but clothed upon, that mortality might be swallowed up of life."
> 2 Corinthians 5:1-4

Paul is referring to the spiritual body that we as believers constantly refer to putting on when we are all "changed". We know that Paul is not talking about housing in the traditional sense because he uses the word *oiketerion* and he ultimately refers to this as clothing so that "we shall not be found naked." As we read further into 1 Corinthians, we find the following statements from Paul:

> "It is sown a natural body; it is raised a spiritual body. There is a natural body, and there is a spiritual body. And so it is written, The first man Adam was made a living soul; the last Adam was made a quickening spirit. Howbeit that was not

> first which is spiritual, but that which is natural; and afterward that which is spiritual. The first man is of the earth, earthy; the second man is the Lord from heaven. As is the earthy, such are they also that are earthy: and as is the heavenly, such are they also that are heavenly. And as we have borne the image of the earthy, we shall also bear the image of the heavenly. Now this I say, brethren, that flesh and blood cannot inherit the kingdom of God; neither doth corruption inherit incorruption. Behold, I shew you a mystery; We shall not all sleep, but we shall all be changed, In a moment, in the twinkling of an eye, at the last trump: for the trumpet shall sound, and the dead shall be raised incorruptible, and we shall be changed." 1 Corinthians 15:44-52

If the physical body can change into a spiritual body, is it possible that a spiritual body can somehow become physical? There are several examples in the Bible of spiritual bodies becoming physical and physical bodies becoming spiritual.

- The Word becomes flesh (John 1:14)
- Jesus becomes a living spirit (1 Cor. 15:45)
- Physical bodies become spiritual bodies (2 Cor. 5:1-4)

The following list is a very small list of shapeshifting beings from other cultures around the world. The idea of a supernatural being that can change shape is not unique to the Bible:

- Greek – Zeus
- Norse – Loki
- Welsh – Arawn
- Armenian – Nhang
- India – Naga
- Tatar – Yuxa
- Philippines – Aswang
- China – Huli Jing
- Japan – Kitsune
- Korea – Kumiho

In our modern culture we have become familiar with many types of movie monsters, but sometimes fail to associate them with shapeshifting:

- Vampires
- Werewolves

- Faeries
- Witches
- Wizards
- Spriggans

In addition to being referred to as Shapeshifters, they are also known by several other names:

- Metamorph
- Skin-Walker
- Mimic
- Therianthrope

There are so many Shapeshifter stories from around the world that all of them could not be listed. The above grouping is just a small sampling of those stories. The fact that there are so many of these stories from cultures that had different religious beliefs lends major credibility to the subject. However, it is important to keep in mind that the majority of these stories revolved around malevolent beings meaning to cause harm to mankind, which is the agenda of the fallen angels.

Angels Can Control The Elements

The idea that the elements can be controlled by beings with power over nature is reflected in movies, video games, TV shows, and books. All of these ideas originate from ancient stories of supernatural beings that display control over the elements in various cultures from around the world. In the Bible, we run into the same concept when we encounter stories of angels that display a mastery over the elements.

> "And after these things I saw four angels standing on the four corners of the earth, holding the four winds of the earth, that the wind should not blow on the earth, nor on the sea, nor on any tree." - Revelation 7:1

Here we have an example of four angels that have control over the wind, and are not allowing it to blow, as a result of a direct command from God. We find similar abilities in other places in scripture as well.

- Fire - Revelation 14:18
- Water - Revelation 16:5

The Bible specifically mentions angels having control over wind, fire, and water, but no direct control over the ground. Control over the ground/earth was given to mankind in Genesis 1:28. In addition to this, the Bible alludes to angels having control over other things as well.

> "He cast upon them the fierceness of his anger, wrath, and indignation, and trouble, by sending evil angels among them." - Psalm 78:49

If we read all of Psalm 78, we see that it is a retelling of the events that happened in Egypt during the Exodus. If we go through the story of the Exodus, it may be implying that angels have control over the following plagues that are not listed above:

- Frogs
- Lice
- Flies
- Death
- Rain
- Hail
- Thunder
- Locust
- Darkness
- Boils

We need to keep in perspective that these angels were acting on behalf of God, so they are referred to as *mal'ak*. Another interesting point made in Psalm 78 is the Hebrew word for evil. The Hebrew word used is *"ra"*. The word does not simply mean evil in the sense that we think of the word. It also means affliction, sorrow, misery, grief, or distress. The irony of the word used here is also not apparent if you are not familiar with ancient Egyptian mythology. Ra was one of the main gods that the Egyptians worshipped. He was believed to control the sun and various sky elements. In essence, God is making a mockery of the Egyptian Ra (sun god) with His *ra mal'ak* (misery angels).

Chapter 6: The Abilities of Angels

The stories of supernatural entities displaying control over the different elements are not unique to the Bible. The following is a very short list of entities from other cultures that are believed to control different elements.

Thunder and Lightning

- Greek – Zeus
- Norse – Thor
- Babylonian – Marduk
- Hittite – Tarhunt
- China – Lei Gong
- Lakota – Haokah

Oceans, Seas, and Rivers

- Aztec – Chalchiuhtlatonal
- Canaanite – Yam
- Irish – Sinann
- Greek – Poseidon
- Egypt – Khnum
- Finnish – Ahti

Fire

- India – Agni
- Babylon – Nergal
- China – Zhu Rong
- Aztec – Xiuhtecuhtli
- Sumer – Gibil
- Akkadian – Ishum

The above list is by no means complete. For example, the Hindu religion alone believes in over 300 million gods that serve different purposes and functions. This again ties into the idea that what they are worshiping as gods are actually the fallen angels of the Bible.

Angels Can Choose To Be Good or Bad

This ability should be self evident based on the fact that Satan is a fallen angel that chose to rebel against God. However, there are some people that teach that angels do not have free will. While most Christians are familiar with the fall of Satan, there is a small, overlooked, verse in which a spirit (not necessarily an angel) volunteers to lie.

> "And there came forth a spirit, and stood before the LORD, and said, I will persuade him. And the LORD said unto him, Wherewith? And he said, I will go forth, and I will be a lying spirit in the mouth of all his prophets. And he said, Thou shalt persuade him, and prevail also: go forth, and do so." - 1 Kings 22:21-22

This spirit, which is likely an angel, volunteers to go down and lie to the prophets. It is also important to note that this may not be an angel, but something else altogether. In addition to this, 1/3 of the angels decided to follow Satan and rebel against God. On the flip side of that, 2/3 chose to continue serving God. Because of this, we know that angels have free will to choose good or evil (Genesis 3:5). According to Paul, angels are also capable of preaching a false gospel (Galatians 1:8). 2 Peter 2:4 tells that some angels have sinned and as a result were locked in chains of darkness. If they did not have free will, none of the above would have been possible.

Angels Can Enter Dreams

People have reported seeing angels in dreams and visions all throughout history. Are these just very graphic hallucinations or something controlled by an outside party? In the Bible we find no less than five references to angels entering dreams:

- Genesis 28:12 (Jacob)
- Genesis 31:11(Jacob)
- Matthew 1:20 (Joseph)
- Matthew 2:13 (Joseph)
- Matthew 2:19 (Joseph)

In the book of Job we find another reference to a spirit entering Job's dream. However, the text does not tell us exactly what this spirit is.

Chapter 6: The Abilities of Angels

> "In thoughts from the visions of the night, when deep sleep falleth on men, Fear came upon me, and trembling, which made all my bones to shake. Then a spirit passed before my face; the hair of my flesh stood up: It stood still, but I could not discern the form thereof: an image was before mine eyes, there was silence, and I heard a voice, saying, Shall mortal man be more just than God? shall a man be more pure than his maker?" - Job 4:13-17

There are some that suspect that this was actually the Holy Spirit appearing to Job in a dream, but the text is unclear as to whether or not that is true.

Angels Can Cross Dimensions

There are several places in the Bible that show angels suddenly appearing all over the place. We see angels moving between heaven and earth (Genesis 28:12), between earth and the underworld (1 Samuel 28), and even into people's dreams (Matthew 2:13). Angels do not seem to be bound to just existing in a single dimensional plane like humans. This crossing of dimensions usually involves a fluctuation of time as well. Encounters that usually involve time fluctuation occur with the following beings:

- Angels
- Fairies
- Extraterrestrials

All of these entities seem to have the same motive for abducting human beings. For a detailed chart of what these beings have in common with the gods, see my book, <u>As The Days of Noah Were</u>.

Angels Can Eat

Most Christians know the story of Moses and the Israelites wandering the desert for forty years. Most of us also know the story of how God fed them with manna during that time. What many people fail to connect is that manna was literally bread from heaven. Who in heaven is eating bread that can also be eaten by humans? According to David, it is the angels.

> "Man did eat angels' food: he sent them meat to the full." - Psalm 78:25

In Genesis we find the Lord and two angels stopping in to eat and drink with Abraham. Abraham was fully aware of who they were. If they were not capable of eating, it is unlikely that Abraham would have bothered offering them food and even more unlikely that they would accept the invitation. After they finish eating, the angels continue to Sodom and then have a meal with Lot and his family.

Angels Have A Military

We know that there was at least one past war in heaven and that there will be at least one future war in heaven. In order to have a war, a military is usually required. While the Bible does not come right out and say that angels have a military, there are references to certain actions that confirm the existence of an angelic military. The best example would be Revelation 12, which depicts a war between Michael, Satan, and their respective armies.

Angels Can Interact With Animals

In the Bible we see angels controlling animals and in at least one encounter, the animal was able to see the angel while the human was not (Numbers 22). After seeing the angel of the Lord standing in the middle of the road, the donkey came to a complete stop, prompting an abusive reaction from Balaam. After this, the angel allows the donkey to speak in human language, which is one of only two occasions in the Bible where animals speak. The other occasion is debatable but it involves the Serpent's conversation with Eve in the Garden of Eden (Genesis 3). In the book of Daniel the angel of the Lord appears in the lion's den and prevents them from killing the prophet. This

Chapter 6: The Abilities of Angels

shows that they have at least some degree of control over otherwise natural instincts of animals.

Angels Can Stop Speech

When Zacharias refused to believe Gabriel about his wife giving birth, he made it so that he was unable to speak (Luke 1). Many people report the inability to speak or make sounds during alien abduction, sleep paralysis, visions of ghosts, and during other supernatural experiences. There are many Christian researchers that believe the intention behind the prevention of speech during an abduction or sleep paralysis experience is to stop the victim from calling out the name of Jesus. Many victims have reported that prayer stops the experience almost immediately.

Angels Escort The Dead

In one story we find an angel escorting Lazarus into Abraham's Bosom, the place where the dead that were faithful to God would go in the Old Testament (Luke 16). Across from Abraham's Bosom is what we would refer to as hell. Other cultures that believe in supernatural beings that would escort the dead to the underworld include the Greeks and Romans, but they were certainly not alone in these beliefs.

Angels Can Cure Sickness

Healing the sick was a big part of Jesus' ministry, but it is something also attributed to at least one angel.

> "For an angel went down at a certain season into the pool, and troubled the water: whosoever then first after the troubling of the water stepped in was made whole of whatsoever disease he had." – John 5:4

Once again, this is another widely held belief by many cultures from around the world. Ancient people would often look to the gods and perform sacrifices in order to obtain favor and healing.

Angels Can Control Objects

Controlling objects without touching them was probably made the most popular by Star Wars, in which the Jedi use the "force" to do all kinds of interesting things. The modern day term for this is telekinesis. In the book of Acts, an angel displays telekinetic ability while freeing Peter from Prison.

> "And, behold, the angel of the Lord came upon him, and a light shined in the prison: and he smote Peter on the side, and raised him up, saying, Arise up quickly. And his chains fell off from his hands." – Acts 12:7

In many extreme cases of hauntings and other supernatural encounters, people report objects floating or flying around the room without being touched. The angels' ability to move objects without touching them may be an explanation of those events.

Angels Can Manipulate Time Perception

One of the main elements in many mythologies and modern day alien abduction reports is the altered perception of time. In some cases people believe they have been gone for minutes but in reality hours have passed. In some cases people believe they have been gone for hours and days have passed. During the temptation of Christ, Satan displays this same ability to manipulate the perception of time.

> "And the devil, taking him up into an high mountain, shewed unto him all the kingdoms of the world in a moment of time." – Luke 4:5

Satan's ability to show Jesus every world empire in a moment once again connects the manipulation of time with an angel.

Angels Can Have Sex

While this is a highly controversial subject for some, the fact remains that the Bible clearly says that angels are capable of having sex. Genesis 6 tells the story of the *b'nai ha Elohim* (sons of God) that had offspring with the *benoth Adam* (daughters of Adam) called Nephilim. The phrase *b'nai ha Elohim* is only used five times in the Old Testament and every single time it refers to angels. The following non-Biblically based reasons are usually used to defend the false Lines of Seth Theory, which states that the sons of God were really the line of Seth and the daughters of Adam (men) were really the line of Cain.

Angels having sex with women does not bring glory to God – That is 100% correct, but neither does the fall of Lucifer, the fall of mankind, Nimrod's rebellion, or Sodom and Gomorrah, yet all of these stories are present in the Bible. Each of these stories also resulted in the punishment of the offending parties.

The word Nephilim was added to the text later – This is easily proven to be false if we read any Hebrew version of the Old Testament (Tanach). Many that make this fabricated argument usually point to the fact that the NIV leaves the word untranslated, but it appears in the KJV as the word "giant". Because of this, they claim it was added later.

Angels cannot have sex – As we discussed above, nowhere in the Bible does it say that fallen angels are incapable of reproduction. The Bible says the "angels of God in heaven" do not marry (Matthew 22:30), but it does not say that they are incapable of reproduction. As we know from biology, marriage is not a biological prerequisite for sex.

Angels are spirits and cannot become physical – The Bible says much to the contrary of this belief. The Bible refers to angels eating, grabbing Lot by the hand, fighting, and much more. People teaching this view have completely ignored or twisted scripture in order to make it fit their beliefs.

The subjects of fallen angels, reproduction with human women, and the birth of the Nephilim are covered in depth in my book, As The Days of Noah Were.

Angels Desire To Learn

According to Peter, there are some things that not even the angels understand. Because they do not understand it they desire to look into at least this very specific matter.

> "Unto whom it was revealed, that not unto themselves, but unto us they did minister the things, which are now reported unto you by them that have preached the gospel unto you with the Holy Ghost sent down from heaven; which things the angels desire to look into." – 1 Peter 1:12

If angels are capable of being curious about humans and the Holy Spirit, it is possible that they are curious and desire to learn about other things as well.

Other Implied Abilities

In addition to the abilities that the Bible comes right out and associates with angels, there are other abilities that are implied by their actions.

Creative Thought: This ability is implied in Galatians 1:8 where Paul refers to the possibility of angels preaching another gospel. Developing an alternative story and possibly an entirely different religion takes creative thought to accomplish.

Invent Technology: The angels have a desire to learn, the fallen ones used genetic interference during the days of Noah, and they flew in vehicles called *merkabah*. The angels seem to have at least some understanding of how things work, so it's not a huge leap to conclude that they are capable of inventing technology.

Having Emotion: In Job 38 the angels shout for joy, which is an emotion. In Revelation 12 Satan comes to pour out his

Chapter 6: The Abilities of Angels

wrath on mankind and wrath is an emotion. Angels do not seem to be mindless, emotionless, beings created by God as many mainstream churches would have us believe.

Please keep in mind that the above statements are just speculation based on what the Bible does tell us. However, it is strongly recommended that you refer to the scriptures for yourself.

Abilities of Angels and Demons

Abilities	Angels	Demons
Free Will	X	X
Good	X	-
Evil	X	X
Appear As Men	X	-
Possess Humans	-	X
Possess Animals	-	X
Control Elements	X	-
Super Strength	X	X
Multiple Voices	-	X
Telekinetic Power	X	-

When we compare the abilities of angels and demons, it quickly become apparent that the only things they have in common are free will and super strength. While the Bible is clear that there are good and bad angels, demons are always presented as doing evil. Why exactly do the majority of churches teach that fallen angels and demons are the same thing? The answer is, probably because they do not bother to do the research and just repeat the accepted traditions of men. The following is a list of beliefs about angels and demons, taught in church, but do not actually appear in the Bible:

- Fallen angels are demons (not in the Bible)
- Fallen angels were stripped of their powers (not in the Bible)
- Angels cannot have sex (not in the Bible)
- Angels are hermaphrodites (not in the Bible)

The major problems with the above teachings are that many Christians do not actually do their own research to insure that what the pastor is teaching is actually in the Bible. Because of this, the tradition is continued and taught as if it is scripture. Perhaps even worse than teaching things that are not in the Bible, as if they are scripture, are teachings that are in complete opposition of scripture.

- Angels do not have free will (opposite of the Bible)
- Angels do not physically manifest (opposite of the Bible)
- Angels do not have a gender (opposite of the Bible)

It is teachings like these that have kept the Church blind to many of the explanations of supernatural events that occur all throughout history. When we begin to understand the context of supernatural experiences in the light of what scripture actually says about supernatural beings, we are no longer able to be deceived into believing that angels are something that they are not.

The Breakdown

The comparisons presented in this chapter were made to show you that the Hebrew Bible is not the only book that contains references to the abilities of the supernatural entities that we call angels. These abilities were not and are not unique to only the good angels, but they are shared by the fallen angels as well. While this study is certainly intriguing, it is important not to get caught up or sucked into angelology because it is an easy topic to get pulled into. My main purpose in writing this chapter is to demonstrate that the angels in the Bible are not allegory, metaphor, simile, or any other figure of speech. They are real beings that were encountered by many cultures throughout history and are likely still being encountered in our modern day. The human interpretation of what these beings are continues to change, but human interpretation does not change what they truly are.

As Christians, our fight is not with flesh and blood, but with supernatural beings referred to as angels and demons. Although demons are not covered in depth in this chapter, they do not seem to be the same thing as angels when compared side by side. You are strongly encouraged to check every statement made in this chapter, but remember to stay covered in prayer because it is easy to be deceived when we stray from using the Bible as our guide and final word in these matters.

Chapter in Review

- Are angels misunderstood?
- What are angels capable of?
- Are fallen angels real?
- Are angels and demons the same thing?
- Do angels have bodies?
- Can angels lie?
- How many angels are there?

Critical Thinking

- Should we study angels?
- Are angels a thing of the past?
- Are angels walking among people now?
- When were angels created?

The Plan of Salvation

The plan of salvation is not difficult or complicated at all. In fact it can be summed up in one single verse. All you need to do in order to be saved is the following:

> That if thou shalt confess with thy mouth the Lord Jesus, and shalt believe in thine heart that God hath raised him from the dead, thou shalt be saved." - Romans 10:9

If you have accepted Christ, your next step should be to get your hands on a King James Version of the Bible. Before joining any church, you should have a good foundation in scripture without the influences of any teacher. Once you have a general understanding of scripture, visit a few churches before deciding on a church home. Make sure you check behind the pastor and do not just accept their word for anything without checking (Acts 17:11). If asking questions is discouraged, steer clear of that church at all costs.

Key Scriptures For Review

- 1 Kings 22
- Job 4
- Psalms 78
- 1 Corinthians 15
- 2 Corinthians 5
- 2 Corinthians 11
- 1 Peter 1
- Jude 1
- Revelation 7

Submit Your Questions

If you have more questions about spiritual warfare, angels, demons, the supernatural, or the Bible in general, you are welcome to submit your questions to me personally. Answers to your questions will be posted as an article on the website for everyone to see.

www.MinisterFortson.com

Chapter 7: The Origin of Demons

> "Three eternal truths: things are not what they seem, the world is at war, and each of us has a crucial role to play" – John Eldredge

Demons are perhaps the most disturbing of all supernatural entities and their ability to inhabit almost anyone or anything makes them extremely difficult to identify. Tradition has taught us that demons were once angels that served God before they rebelled and chose follow Lucifer. According to church tradition, following their rebellion, they were stripped of their powers, ability to appear in a human form, and were cursed to look for bodies to inhabit, but this story is absolutely nowhere to be found in the Bible. Even more peculiar than these non-Biblical stories being passed around in the Church, are the people that cling to these traditions as if they are scripture. When we use the Bible to do a side by side comparison of angels and demons, we find many differences in both the names and abilities of these entities.

Names of Angels and Demons

Names	Angels	Demons
Elohim	X	-
Malak	X	-
Shed	-	X
Sa'iyr	-	X
Aggelos/Angelos	X	-
Daimon	-	X

Since we have already taken an in depth look at the words *elohim* and *mal'ak*, let's start by looking at the Hebrew words for demon, *shed* and *sa'iyr*. These two words have a very significant amount of history behind them and may reveal many of the commonly held Church traditions to be false. Both of the words used for demon in the Old Testament are only used twice, and neither of the two fit the Biblical description of a fallen angel.

Hybridization and Demons

In other non-Biblical texts that are important to Jewish history, we find a strange reference to the creation of different types of hybrids and their possible connection to the demons of the Bible. The following quote is taken from the book of Jubilees.

> "The Sons of God were sent down to teach mankind truth and justice; and for three hundred years did indeed teach Cain's son Enoch all the secrets of Heaven and Earth. Later, however, they lusted after mortal women and defiled themselves by sexual intercourse. Enoch has recorded not only their divine instructions, but also their subsequent fall from grace; before the end they were indiscriminately enjoying virgins, matrons, men, and beasts." - Jubilees 4:15, 22, 5:1

As Christians we have to ask, "Is there any Biblical basis for believing these stories?" If we take a closer look at the Bible, we will soon see that not all of these stories are made up and there may be more truth to them than we ever realized.

The Origin of The Shed

The *shed* were well known throughout the Middle East as powerful spirits. The first place in the Bible that we encounter the *shed* is in reference to Israel worshiping them.

> "They sacrificed unto devils (*Shed*), not to God; to gods whom they knew not, to new gods that came newly up, whom your fathers feared not." - Deuteronomy 32:17

The deeper we look into the words of Moses, the stranger the entire verse becomes. The first thing that we notice is that sacrifices are being made to these *shed* by the Israelites. The second aspect to this strange scenario is that Moses points out that these were new "gods" that their fathers did not fear. In order to keep this in perspective, we have to remember that the Israelites had just been freed from Egypt, where they worshipped many different gods. The shed were completely differ-

Chapter 7: The Origin of Demons

ent than the gods that were worshiped in Egypt. Moses also tells us that they were "new gods that came newly up".

- *Chadash* (Hebrew) – New thing, something new.

Not only were the Hebrews sacrificing to these *shed*, Moses points out that their fathers did not fear them. This seems to imply that the Israelites may have had a genuine fear of the *shed* that did not exist in previous generations. Let's take a look at the word used for fear in Hebrew.

- *Sa'ar* (Hebrew) – to shiver, to be horribly afraid.

The Israelites were much more than scared; the English equivalent to the word *sa'ar* would be terrified. Not only were they terrified, but it is in the book of Psalms that we find out just how terrified they were and what kind of sacrifices they were making to the *Shed*.

> "Yea, they sacrificed their sons and their daughters unto devils," – Psalm 106:37

The Israelites were so scared that they began to sacrifice their own sons and daughters. What kind of entity would make a person so fearful that they would kill their own flesh and blood in a sacrifice? Unfortunately, the Bible does not give us a description of these beings, but there was another culture in the area, that worshiped the *shed* and kept very detailed records of them, including carvings and depictions.

The Assyrians and Babylonians worshiped creatures known as the *shedu*. Both cultures were closely connected and spoke the Semitic language Akkadian, which was very similar to ancient Hebrew. According to the beliefs at the time, the *lamassu* (female) and the *shedu* (male) were the same creature. These beings were depicted in the following manner:

Stone Carving of Assyrian Shedu

According to the Assyrian and Babylonian cultures, the *shedu* were hybrids with the body of a bull, wings of an eagle, and the head of a man. Stories of hybrid creatures generally appear in two time periods: very ancient history and modern times. As we continue digging into the origin of demons, we will see that there is a very strong connection between demons and hybrid creatures.

The Origin of The Sa'iyr

The *sa'iyr* are an interesting group of spiritual beings because, like the *shed*, they too were considered to be hybrids. Here is how the Strong's Concordance defines the word *sa'iyr*:

- *sa'iyr* (Hebrew) – Satyr, Faun, He-Goat, Shaggy

The origin of the word *sa'iyr* is *sa'ar* (to shiver, be horribly afraid). Stories of fauns and satyrs are most prominent in the

Chapter 7: The Origin of Demons

myths and legends of other cultures, but here we find a reference to the same creatures in the Old Testament. So what exactly are Fauns and Satyrs?

> "The faun is a half human - half goat (from the head to the waist being the human half, but with the addition of goat's horns) manifestation of forest and animal spirits which would help or hinder humans at whim. Romans believed fauns inspired fear in men traveling in lonely, remote or wild places."[1]

As we have seen, the origins of the satyr belief has its root in the Hebrew word for fear. Over a thousand years later, the Romans held the same belief that these hybrid creatures struck fear in the hearts of men that traveled alone. The Hebrews feared these creatures and as a result, also worshiped and made sacrifices to them.

> "And they shall no more offer their sacrifices unto devils, after whom they have gone a whoring. This shall be a statute for ever unto them throughout their generations." – Leviticus 17:7

---

[1] http://en.wikipedia.org/wiki/Faun

The words God uses, while speaking to Moses, in the above verse are interesting because it provides a link between the *sa'iyr* and another legend surrounding these creatures. God refers to the people "whoring" after the *sa'iyr*. The Hebrew word used is *zanah*, which is translated as prostitute, whore, whoring, and fornication in the Old Testament. Much of the Church teaching on fornication has been diluted down to only mean sex. However, throughout the Bible, there is a strong connection between fornication and pagan worship. In every legend of Fauns and Satyrs, they are well known for their sexual escapades with human women and sometimes men.

> "Satyrs are described as roguish but faint-hearted folk, subversive and dangerous, yet shy and cowardly. As Dionysiac creatures they are lovers of wine and women, and they are ready for every physical pleasure."[2]

Among the list of activities in satyr mythology, is their associating with music, dancing, playfulness, and orgies. The Old Testament actually contains a reference that associates the satyr with dancing.

> "But wild beasts of the desert shall lie there; and their houses shall be full of doleful creatures; and owls shall dwell there, and satyrs shall dance there." - Isaiah 13:21

The word translated as satyrs in the above verse is the same word translated as devils in Leviticus 17:7. This leads us back to the question, "were stories of these creatures more than just myth and legend?" As we continue digging into the *sa'iyr*, we encounter one in particular that is said to be the origin of the word pandemonium.

> "Pan aided his foster-brother in the battle with the Titans by letting out a horrible screech and scattering them in terror."[3]

According to legend, it was this scream of Pan that led to pan-demonium among his rivals. The Greek word *daimonium* refers to being under the influence of a demon. Pandemonium literally translates as "under the demonic control of Pan". The

---

[2] http://en.wikipedia.org/wiki/Satyr
[3] http://en.wikipedia.org/wiki/Pan_%28god%29#Mythology

Chapter 7: The Origin of Demons

story of Pan is linked to a great battle for the heavens in the Greek culture, but when we look deeper into the Hebrew culture, we find a similar story of a fallen angel by the name of Azazel. The name Azazel was used in the movie, Fallen, starring Denzel Washington. In the movie, Azazel was presented as woodland demon that had the power to possess humans and animals. Surprisingly, we find mention of Azazel in the Bible in association with sin and goats.

> "And Aaron shall cast lots upon the two goats; one lot for the LORD, and the other lot for the scapegoat." – Leviticus 16:8

It is important to point out that this particular goat was not the fallen angel in question. The Hebrew word translated as scapegoat is Azazel, which means, "the goat that has gone astray." The story of Azazel is actually a very old Hebrew belief that does not come from the Bible, but from events that they believe happened prior to Noah's flood.

> "Azazel is represented in the Book of Enoch as one of the leaders of the rebellious Watchers in the time preceding the flood; he taught men the art of warfare, of making swords, knives, shields, and coats of mail, and women the art of deception by ornamenting the body, dying the hair, and painting the face and the eyebrows, and also revealed to the people the secrets of witchcraft and corrupted their manners, leading them into wickedness and impurity; until at last he was, at the Lord's command, bound hand and foot by the archangel Raphael and chained to the rough and jagged rocks of [Ha] Duduael (= Beth Ḥadudo), where he is to abide in utter darkness until the great Day of Judgment, when he will be cast into the fire to be consumed forever."[4]

This particular belief comes from 1 Enoch, which was hidden in Qumran, along with other books of the Bible. 1 Enoch also appears in the Ethiopian Bible and many other early translations. It was also a very popular book during the 2nd Temple period, and is referenced by Peter, Jude, and John in Revelation. While it is not considered scripture, both Jews and early Christians considered this book to be a very important book that reflected early beliefs about Noah's flood. Did the crea-

---

[4] Enoch viii. 1, ix. 6, x. 4-6, liv. 5, lxxxviii. 1; see Geiger, "Jüd. Zeit." 1864, pp. 196-204

tion of Satyrs begin with a fallen angel that rebelled against God? While we cannot say for sure, it seems to fit the motive of fallen angels that want to corrupt all of God's creation.

The Origin of The Nephilim

In my book, <u>As The Days of Noah Were</u>, there is a very in depth chapter on the Nephilim, so this section will very briefly cover the subject. Much of what we know about the Nephilim comes from Genesis 6:1-4. Nephilim is translated in the KJV as "giants", and they are all over the Bible.

Individual Nephilim

- Ahiman - Son of Anak
- Agag - King of The Amalekites
- Anak - Father of the Anakim
- Arba - Father of Anak
- Goliath - A Philistine Warrior
- Ishbibenob - Goliath's Brother
- Lahmi - Goliath's Brother
- Og - King of Bashan
- Saph - Goliath's Brother
- Sheshai - Son of Anak
- Sihon - King of The Amorites
- Talmai - Son of Anak

Tribes of Nephilim

- Emim
- Rephaim
- Anakim
- Zamzummim
- Amalekites
- Amorites

It was the presence of these hybrids that caused Moses to hesitate entering the Promised Land after hearing the account of the spies in Numbers 13:33. Saul allowed the *nephilim* king Agag to live instead of killing him as God commanded; this led to Saul losing the throne in 1 Samuel 15, and according to the

Chapter 7: The Origin of Demons

book of Enoch, these hybrids also turned into demons upon death.

> "And now, **the giants, who are produced from the spirits and flesh, shall be called evil spirits upon the earth**, and on the earth shall be their dwelling. Evil spirits have proceeded from their bodies; because **they are born from men and from the holy Watchers** is their beginning and primal origin; **they shall be evil spirits on earth, and evil spirits shall they be called**. [As for the spirits of heaven, in heaven shall be their dwelling, but as for the spirits of the earth which were born upon the earth, on the earth shall be their dwelling.] And the spirits of the giants afflict, oppress, destroy, attack, do battle, and work destruction on the earth, and cause trouble: they take no food, but nevertheless hunger and thirst, and cause offences. And **these spirits shall rise up against the children of men and against the women**, because they have proceeded from them." - Enoch 15:8-12

Again, Enoch is not scripture but it does give us one more historical reference to hybrids being associated with the origin of demons, and demonstrates that the Bible is not the only book to mention these types of hybrids. They are also found in Greek mythology as well, and are referred to as demigods. The creation of a demigod happens when a god (fallen angel) descends from the sky, has sex with a human woman, and produces a hybrid offspring. These offspring later become famous, and legendary stories are written about them. Here are a few familiar demigods from mythology:

- Hercules
- Perseus
- Achilles
- Gilgamesh

This belief in hybrid god-men was partly responsible for Hitler's actions during WWII. It was not the belief by itself that was bad, but Hitler's belief that he could get the god-men to return through means of human sacrifice. As we learned previously, the worship of these hybrids included human sacrifices. Quite a few cultures also participated in human sacrifice as part of their worship of the god-men:

- Mayans
- Babylonians
- Greeks
- Hebrews
- Assyrians

"The wicked emperor Hadrian, who conquered Jerusalem, boasted, 'I have conquered Jerusalem with great power.' Rabbi Johanan ben Zakkai said to him, 'Do not boast. Had it not been the will of Heaven, you would not have conquered it.' Rabbi Johanan then took Hadrian into a cave and showed him the bodies of Amorites who were buried there. One of them measured eighteen cubits [approximately 30 feet] in height. He said, 'When we were deserving, such men were defeated by us, but now, because of our sins, you have defeated us" (quoted in *Judaism*, edited by Arthur Hertzberg, p.155-156, George Braziller, New York: 1962)

Interestingly enough, we are just getting started with what both the Bible and history have to say about the hybrids that were once part of every culture on earth. We are now going to look at a few very interesting references to other hybrids in the Bible.

The Legend of The Minotaur

According to the Greek's there was a hybrid creature known as the Minotaur (Minos' Bull). It was a bull/human hybrid that had a taste for human flesh. In order to keep it appeased, they would sacrifice humans to it. The question we have to ask is, "is there any truth to this story?" Many people believe this story is just another myth among many, but it has several things in common with scripture:

- This creature came about as a result of the "gods" tampering/experimenting with humans and animals.
- Human sacrifices were made to this creature.
- This creature was being worshiped out of fear.

Although it is not well known among the general population, the Minotaur actually had a name. The name given to the hybrid at birth was Asterion, which means "ruler of the stars". This was also the name of Minos' father. The story of the Minotaur provides an interesting reference to the gods' involvement in the creation of animal human hybrids, but what, if anything, does the Bible say about such a creature?

The Abomination of The Ammonites

The Ammonites and the Moabites both worshiped a creature that many believe to be the same, but with two different names. The Moabites referred to it as Chemosh and the Ammonites referred to it as Molech/Moloch. The Bible, however, refers to both Chemosh and Molech as abominations.

> "Then did Solomon build an high place for Chemosh, the abomination of Moab, in the hill that is before Jerusalem, and for Molech, the abomination of the children of Ammon." - 1 Kings 11:7

Sunday School level Bible teaching usually conditions us to believe that these were just idols that were being worshiped, but actual research and study reveals a completely different story. The following is a description of how Molech/Chemosh was depicted:

> "Then further back, higher than the candelabrum, and much higher than the altar, rose the Moloch, all of iron, and with gaping apertures in his human breast. His outspread wings were stretched upon the wall, his tapering hands reached down to the ground; three black stones bordered by yellow circles represented three eyeballs on his brow, **and his bull's head was raised with a terrible effort as if in order to bellow.**" - Salammbo (Gustave Flaubert)

In the above description, Molech/Chemosh has the head of a bull, arms like a man, and wings. It actually sounds very similar to the Assyrian shedu. In order to really get a good idea of how the Minotaur (left) and Molech (right) were depicted, here are two side by side pictures:

According to Jeremiah 32:35, the children of Israel began to worship Molech by sacrificing their children to him. They would build alters in his image, like in the picture above, light a fire, and toss in their children. This tradition continued into New Testament times, where they would sacrifice people inside of a brass bull in honor of Zeus, who played a role in the creation of the Minotaur, according to the Greeks. The connection between the Greek Minotaur and Molech might just be an interesting coincidence if it was not for several more occurrences of this same creature in other cultures:

- Apis – Egypt
- Sarangay – Philippines
- Ushi-oni – Japan

It is entirely possible, but not likely that all of these cultures made up the exact same creature and gave it the exact same origin by coincidence, but it is highly unlikely since they all had different religions, social, political, and economic situations. As we continue this journey we are going to encounter several stranger hybrid creatures mentioned in the Bible.

Chapter 7: The Origin of Demons

Hybrids Worthy of Mention

So far we have looked at the Shedu, Sa'iyr, Nephilim, and Molech, but there are still at least three more hybrid creatures in the Bible that we have not looked at:

- Lion Men of Moab (2 Samuel 23:20)
- Living Creatures/Cherubim (Ezekiel 1 & 10)
- Locust From The Pit (Revelation 9)

In my book, <u>As The Days of Noah Were</u>, there is a much deeper study on the Lion Men of Moab and the Cherubim, so we are going to focus on the locusts from the pit in this section. According to Revelation, the locusts from the pit are described as follows:

> "And the shapes of the locusts were like unto horses prepared unto battle; and on their heads were as it were crowns like gold, and their faces were as the faces of men. And they had hair as the hair of women, and their teeth were as the teeth of lions. And they had breastplates, as it were breastplates of iron; and the sound of their wings was as the sound of chariots of many horses running to battle. And they had tails like unto scorpions, and there were stings in their tails: and their power was to hurt men five months." – Revelation 9:7-10

The picture above is a very close match to the description in Revelation 9, with the exception of the missing crown. Strangely enough, the above picture was not drawn based on the creature in Revelation. It was based on a description of a Persian creature known as the Manticore, which means "man eater". It was called that because it only attacked humans, just like the locusts in Revelation 9. This same creature also appears in the legends of India and Greece, but why? Now that we have a brief understanding of the history of hybrids, let's look at how it ties in to modern times.

The Transhumanist Agenda

Transhumanism is a modern word that describes the scientific pursuit of becoming more than human. It is a combination of the words Transcend and Human. This pursuit usually involves the blending of human and animal DNA in order to create something that is not fully human, but not fully animal. Although the word is new, as we can see from above, the concept is very old and reflected in almost every culture on earth. For those of us that put our faith in the Bible, the pursuit of hybrid creature should be expected.

> "The thing that hath been, it is that which shall be; and that which is done is that which shall be done: and there is no new thing under the sun." – Ecclesiastes 1:9

Many people do not consider Ecclesiastes to be a prophetic book, but it is. In the opening chapter we learn that there is nothing new under the sun. As we dig into the origins of the Transhumanist movement, we find that to be the case. Humanity's past is filled with stories of hybrids, and there are people now attempting to revive those hybrids from our present. One of the creatures scientists are attempting to re-create is the Minotaur. Last year (2011) there was a BBC News report in which scientist shared their desire to create a cow/human hybrid. In other words, they want to re-create the Minotaur. This BBC News video, announcing the project, can be found on my website under the article, *Return of the Minotaur: Science Fact or Science Fiction*.

Chapter 7: The Origin of Demons

This is a subject that the mainstream church is not taking seriously or is completely ignoring. This policy of burying our head in the sand is leaving people without Biblical answers to a very Biblical situation, and as a result, people are seeking answers outside of the church. Once the Church denies or ignores a situation, it gives the secular Transhumanists an opportunity to indoctrinate those seekers with their beliefs and ideals. The only way for the Church to counter this is through first educating ourselves, and then educating others as to the real dangers of our current scientific pursuits. The following is a brief list of animal/human hybrids that are public knowledge:

- Mouse/Human
- Pig/Human
- Sheep/Human
- Rabbit/Human

According to official reports, these hybrids were not allowed to grow to maturity, but the actions of state governments is pointing to something different and possibly even more sinister. To date, three states have made it a felony to knowingly create an animal/human hybrid and a misdemeanor to knowingly purchase one. Those states are:

- Arizona
- Louisiana
- Ohio

One could argue that the Human-Animal Hybrid Prohibition Act is a preventative law, but notice that it is a misdemeanor to buy a hybrid. The fact is people break the law and it is almost inevitable that someone will grow a hybrid to maturity and there will be a demand for it. Because of the illegal nature, these hybrids will become very high priced black market items, making their creators extremely rich.

Germline and Somatic Parahumans

Germline Parahumans are what we are referring to when we talk about Nephilim, demigods, and animal human hybrids. It refers to a hybrid that is modified or created before the birthing process.

"Another key difference is that a germ-line parahuman would have to be modified before birth, while a somatic parahuman could be an adult human who chooses to be modified."[5]

If the phrase "somatic parahumans" is unfamiliar to you, it may become very familiar in the near future. On the TV show *Heroes*, they developed an injection that gave ordinary people super powers of their choosing. The scientific study of somatic parahumans would do the exact same thing, but it would alter human DNA and combine it with animal traits. This idea is appealing to many people because it eliminates the need to create hybrids in a lab. Adult human beings could be turned into animal/human hybrids through an injection. Jesus made the following reference to what the end of the age would be like:

> "But as the days of Noah were so shall the coming of the son of man be." – Matthew 24:37

If we go back to the Old Testament and read about the events preceding the flood, we find a very strange statement made by God about the condition of all life on the planet.

> "The earth also was corrupt before God, and the earth was filled with violence. And God looked upon the earth, and, behold, it was corrupt; for all flesh had corrupted his way upon the earth." – Genesis 6:11-12

The ability to create somatic parahumans should be very disturbing to anyone that follows Bible prophecy. Many people discount the End Time Hybrid Hypothesis because they do not see how there would be enough time to contaminate animals and humanity to the point that it was during the time of Noah. This corruption of all flesh could easily be achieved very quickly through the distribution of vaccines or a simple visit to the doctor's office. Jesus gave us a strange warning during the Olivet Discourse that many of the top researchers believe refers

---

[5] http://en.wikipedia.org/wiki/Parahuman

Chapter 7: The Origin of Demons

to nuclear weapons, but as we are starting to see, that may not be the case:

> "And except those days should be shortened, there should no flesh be saved: but for the elect's sake those days shall be shortened." – Matthew 24:22

It is possible that we are once again looking at the coming corruption of all flesh, just as it was during the days of Noah. The major difference between our time and the time of Noah is that many believe the events during Noah's time were involuntary. In our age of media and pop culture, people will line up to receive eagle like eye sight, bear like strength, or any other potential "enhancements" that scientists can think up. This time around, the corruption of all flesh may be voluntary, depending on how the marketing package is put together. All flesh had become corrupted, and that reference does not just apply to humans. It actually applies to humans, animals, and the fallen angels that were responsible for the birth of the Nephilim.

Somatic Parahumans and The Mark

It always seemed strange that simply accepting The Mark of The Beast is an unforgivable sin. According to Revelation 14:9-10, whoever takes the mark will be cast alive into the Lake of Fire. Why would there be such a harsh punishment for taking the mark? This is speculation, but there may be something far more sinister to the mark than previously assumed. Many of the previous theories assert that the mark will be a tattoo, microchip, or barcode of some kind, and some people even believe that it is an ideology. There is now an additional possibility, and that is that the mark will alter human DNA. Christ came as a man to redeem all mankind. This is the spiritual milk that we all learn before coming to know Christ. The reason it is important is because Christ did not become an animal/human hybrid to save animal/human hybrids.

Theory: If the mark is combined with somatic parahumans injections, and people may literally make themselves unredeemable by turning themselves into animal/human hybrids. Receiving this injection would make humans part beast, giving the phrase "mark of the beast" an entirely literal meaning. This is all the more reason to take Matthew 24:22 very literally.

The Corruption of All Flesh

The problem with our understanding of Genesis 6 is largely due to relying completely on the English translation in combination with Church tradition. The word "corrupt" as used in Genesis 6:11-12 actually has no reference to morality.

- Shachath (Hebrew) – destroyed, ruined, blemished, jeopardized, ravaged, spoiled, wasted.

The purpose of the flood was not to destroy the Earth, as we can see from the Hebrew definition of the word corrupt. The Earth was already being destroyed. If God's intent was to completely wipe out all life, there would have been no need to spare Noah, his family, or any of the animals on the ark. Many people take the references to flesh in Genesis 6 to only refer to humans, but it is through the New Testament writer Paul that we get an entirely new perspective of what flesh really is. In 1 Corinthians 15:39-40 Paul tells us that there are five types of flesh:

- Men
- Beasts
- Fish
- Birds
- Celestial/Heavenly

We know the first four were present on earth starting in Genesis 1, but the celestial/heavenly flesh does not arrive on earth until Genesis 6 (sons of God). It is through the writings of Paul that we find out that this "celestial flesh" can be put on by believers like clothing:

> "For we know that if our earthly house of this tabernacle were dissolved, we have a building of God, an house not made with hands, eternal in the heavens. For in this we groan, earnestly desiring to be clothed upon with our house

Chapter 7: The Origin of Demons

> which is from heaven: If so be that being clothed we shall not be found naked." - 2 Corinthians 5:1-3

In this verse, Paul uses the Greek word *oiketerion*, which refers to a spiritual body, thus the reference to us not being found "naked". This is the first of only two times that this word is used in the Bible. This first instance of the word is in reference to believers putting on our new bodies or "celestial flesh". The second mention of the word *oiketerion* occurs in Jude in reference to the angels actually removing this "celestial flesh" from themselves.

> "And the angels which kept not their first estate, but left their own habitation, he hath reserved in everlasting chains under darkness unto the judgment of the great day." - Jude 1:6

Here we see that the angels left their "own habitation" and are reserved in chains of darkness until judgment. We know that Satan was not bound and will not be bound until the end (Revelation 20:1-3), so what is Jude referring to? Jude is actually referencing an event that is only found in the book of Enoch, in which God commands the offending angels to be bound for 70 generations. This subject is covered in depth in my book, <u>As The Days of Noah Were</u>, so it will not be represented here. The point is that these angels corrupted their spiritual flesh and then descended to corrupt the terrestrial flesh, thus God made the statement that all flesh had become corrupt.

Jude goes on to compare the sin of these angels to the sin in Sodom and Gomorrah, which was partly of a sexual nature. Keep in mind, that even with all of the homosexuality that was going on in the city, God still told Abraham that He would spare it for the sake of only ten righteous people (Genesis 18:32). The final straw was the attempted rape of the angels that came to inspect the city. Usually when this subject is taught, it is completely avoided or ignored that if it was impossible to rape these angels, Lot would not have gone out to plead with the crowd, offered them his daughters, or put himself in danger. During the event, the angels intervened and immediately removed Lot and his family from the city. The sexual interaction between the spiritual realm and the natural realm is something that God takes very seriously.

It is my personal opinion that Sodom, Gomorrah, and the two other cities on the plain were destroyed because of their attempted sexual interaction with angels because God was willing to forgive them and spare the cities before this event happened. It is also my personal opinion that it will be the blending of the spiritual and physical realms that will ultimately lead to the Second Coming of Christ.

The Testimony of Scripture

Scripture is always the best interpreter of scripture, so it is important to see what the scripture says about demons. It may surprise you to find out that there is a very widely read verse that may actually point to the very origin and nature of demons.

> "And when he had called unto him his twelve disciples, he gave them power against unclean spirits, to cast them out, and to heal all manner of sickness and all manner of disease." - Matthew 10:1

The Greek word translated as "unclean" actually has a very strange meaning, which seems to confirm the theory of the hybrid origin of demons. The word used is *akathartos*, which means:

> "not pure (because mixed), i.e. adulterated with "a wrong mix" and hence "unclean" (because tainted by sin)." - Strong's #169.

The antonym of this word is *kathairo*, which means "free from wrong mixture." This choice of word usage seems to indicate that demons are indeed some kind of "wrong mixture", just as the hybrid origin theory suggests.

Chapter 7: The Origin of Demons

A Pattern of Intervention

In my book, <u>As The Days of Noah Were</u>, there is a section which explores the various patterns in scripture by which we can predict future spiritual actions. In this section we are going to look at the pattern of God's direct intervention in the form of complete and utter destruction.

> **Example 1:** Noah's flood. The sons of God corrupt the human race and hybrids are introduced into the world. The result is God wiping everything out with a flood and only sparing a select few.
>
> **Example 2:** Sodom and Gomorrah side with the Rephaim, Emimim, and other well known hybrid tribes. When the angels enter the city, the men attempt to rape them and God wipes out the cities, only sparing a select few.
>
> **Example 3:** God commands the Hebrews to take the Promised Land, but ten of the spies give a report of Nephilim in the land. As a result that generation dies off. Joshua and Caleb later take the "Valley of the Giants" wiping out every single hybrid in the area.
>
> **Example 4:** The Nephilim reemerge in the days of David. God commands Saul to wipe out Agag and his entire tribe, which Saul fails to do and as a result loses the throne. David kills Goliath and later David's men kill Goliath's four brothers.

As we can see, there are at least four examples in the Bible of God's direct intervention or command to wipe out these celestial/terrestrial hybrids. The next question is, "is there any indication that this will happen again?" Many people, including myself believe there is plenty of indication in the Bible that this will occur again.

> "And whereas thou sawest iron mixed with miry clay, **they shall mingle themselves with the seed of men**: but they shall not cleave one to another, even as iron is not mixed with clay." – Daniel 2:43

Who are they that will mingle with the seed of men? If this subject is new to you, you need to really consider that question. This prophecy is in reference to end time activity. Many people believe it is a direct reference back to the issue that occurred during the days of Noah, involving the fallen angels. This reference in Daniel is covered in depth in my book, As The Days of Noah Were.

No Holds Barred Warfare

In the beginning chapters of Genesis we see that spiritual warfare manifests itself as attacks on the flesh. In Genesis 3, the Serpent convinces Eve to destroy her flesh by disobeying God and eating the fruit. She then gave it to Adam, who was not deceived (1 Timothy 2:14), and he intentionally destroys his own flesh by eating the fruit. We then see the events that happen during the days of Noah, which led to the corruption of human, animal, and angelic flesh. There are also the subsequent issues in the Sodom, Gomorrah, The Promised Land, Hebron, Gath, and several other places. Then there are the sacrifices of human flesh to the gods in many cultures, but why do we have all of these attacks on the flesh?

> "What? know ye not that your body is the temple of the Holy Ghost which is in you, which ye have of God, and ye are not your own?" - 1 Corinthians 6:19

Satan's issue with God has existed long before the creation of mankind. Many people believe that the first rebellion happened during a "gap" between Genesis 1:1 and Genesis 1:2, which caused the earth to become without form and void. The Gap Theory is briefly covered in my book, As The days of Noah Were. It is after this supposed gap that we find the Spirit of God (Holy Spirit) hovering over the face of the deep in a protective fashion. This was very real spiritual warfare.

Many people believe that Ezekiel 28 is a reference to the fall of Satan. In Ezekiel 28:18 we find that Satan defiled the heavenly sanctuary. If the things on earth are merely a foreshadow or a reflection of what is in heaven, then we know that the Spirit of God dwells in the sanctuary. In Exodus He dwelled in the Tabernacle and when the Temple was built, He dwelled there, which may be why Satan has a history of attacking and defiling

Chapter 7: The Origin of Demons

the Temple. It is my opinion that most of (not all) Satan's attacks are specifically focused at the Holy Spirit while the other fallen angels and demons focus their attacks on everything else, but how was that conclusion reached?

In addition to the attacks on the Temple, we also see that Satan does not attempt to tempt Jesus until after the Holy Spirit descends on Him and leads Him into the wilderness (Matthew 4:1). During the temptation of Christ, Satan quotes from Psalm 91, which is a prophecy concerning the Messiah. According to the Bible, who is responsible for Biblical prophecy?

> "For the prophecy came not in old time by the will of man: but holy men of God spake as they were moved by the Holy Ghost." - 2 Peter 1:21

Satan chose to use the words written by people that were inspired by the Holy Spirit. This attack was well thought out and intentional, otherwise, it would not have been referred to as a temptation. Keep in mind that Jesus was not tempted with the same things that us normal humans are tempted with. He was tempted to use His "God power" in some cases and even offered leadership of the entire world in exchange for worshiping Satan. These attacks seem to be directly focused on offending and disrespecting the Holy Spirit. It was also this specific disrespect of the Holy Spirit that will lead to Satan's ultimate punishment in the Lake of Fire.

> "But he that shall blaspheme against the Holy Ghost hath never forgiveness, but is in danger of eternal damnation." - Mark 3:29

In the Genesis 3, Satan has already turned against God and according to scripture, even his previous rebellion did not result in damnation. He was not sentenced to be destroyed until after he convinced Adam and Eve to commit suicide by eating the fruit. In essence, he was responsible for defiling the temple.

> "If any man defile the temple of God, him shall God destroy; for the temple of God is holy, which temple ye are." - 1 Corinthians 3:17

Everything we are looking at today in terms of hybridization and transhumanism, in my opinion, is linked to Satan's ongoing pattern of disrespecting the Holy Spirit. The Holy Spirit dwells with humans, not animal/human hybrids or angel/human hybrids. In my opinion, animal/human hybrids and angel/human hybrids cannot be saved, and there is no evidence in scripture that they can be. There are people that believe different, but to date there is not a single example in history, mythology, or the Bible of a hybrid wanting to come to salvation through Christ.

We as Christians need to be aware of what is really going on when we hear stories of alien/human hybrids or animal/human hybrids coming across our TV sets. In my opinion, what people believe to be aliens are really fallen angels up to their old tactics as they have always been all throughout the Bible. Hybridization and Transhumanism will likely lead to the creation of demonic spirits as it is believed to have happen during the days of Noah and if we are not careful, we could fall for the lie that all of this is just for the good of mankind.

Pop Culture and Demonic Influence

Recently there has been a lot of focus on symbols used in popular songs by popular artists, but this section is not about any of that. Demonic influence on the entertainment industry has been around for a very long time, but many people may not realize where much of what we find entertaining originates from. We have briefly covered the origin of the giant mythology, so now we will talk about a few lesser known facts that appear in some of our favorite movies.

- Sleep Paralysis
- Vampires
- Zombies

Sleep Paralysis, also known as Night Terrors is a phenomenon that has been going on for thousands of years. One movie that focused entirely on this concept was, THEY. Sleep Paralysis can happen at any time of the day, but usually occurs in the middle of the night. While science offers an explanation that seems to

Chapter 7: The Origin of Demons

make sense, they have yet to offer an explanation as to why people experience an evil presence or see entities in the room with them. The two entities that are commonly reported are the Old Hag and the Man in the Top Hat. In the Bible, Job has an experience with a presence in his room in the middle of the night:

> "In thoughts from the visions of the night, when deep sleep falleth on men, Fear came upon me, and trembling, which made all my bones to shake. Then a spirit passed before my face; the hair of my flesh stood up: It stood still, but I could not discern the form thereof: an image was before mine eyes, there was silence, and I heard a voice, saying, Shall mortal man be more just than God? shall a man be more pure than his maker?" – Job 4:13-17

We are never told whether or not this is a good spirit or a bad spirit, but we are told that it is definitely a spirit. The message that the spirit gives him gives us no clues as to the spirit's intent. What is important is that Job describes this taking place during the middle of the night, his hair standing up on his flesh, and the silence in the room. Quite a few people that have reported experiencing sleep paralysis claim that it can be stopped through prayer and pleading the blood of Christ.

The Origin of Zombies

Zombie movies have been a cash cow for Hollywood studios and video game makers for decades. The idea of people coming back from the dead and devouring the flesh of uninfected humans is both intriguing and disturbing all at the same time. In every bit of fiction there is a bit of reality, and in the case of zombies, truth is definitely stranger than fiction. The basic premise behind a zombie is that a dead person can come back to life, usually as the result of some kind of scientific experiment gone wrong. In Voodoo, a zombie can be created and controlled by a *bokor*, also known as a sorcerer. In Africa, zombies are widely believed in and can be created with the use of various powders. Many books have been written on this widely held African belief, but interestingly the Bible also makes references to these strange beings.

Biblical Zombies

One of the tribes of the Nephilim was known as the Rephaim. The name means, "dead ones, ghosts, or shades". These hybrids were literally, "the walking dead". Isaiah 26:14 in the Hebrew makes it clear that they will have no part in the resurrection. These Biblical zombies may also be the source of the flesh eating lore that surrounds many of the zombie stories. Many of the legends surrounding the Nephilim portray them as evil giants that devoured human flesh. Over time the zombie legend has evolved into what we now see in the Resident Evil video game and move series.

Banned From The Resurrection

According to Isaiah, the giants will not take part in the resurrection. If there was nothing strange or abnormal about the giants in the Bible, there would not be a reason for them to be excluded from the resurrection of the dead. The following three references to Isaiah 26:14 are from the Latin Vulgate, Douay-Rheims, and Young's translations of Isaiah 26:14

> "morientes non vivant gigantes non resurgant propterea visitasti et contrivisti eos et perdidisti omnem memoriam eorum" - Apocalypsis 22:21 Latin: Biblia Sacra Vulgata

> "Let not the dead live, let not the giants rise again: therefore hast thou visited and destroyed them, and best destroyed all their memory." - Douay-Rheims Bible

> "Dead -- they live not, Rephaim, they rise not, Therefore Thou hast inspected and dost destroy them, Yea, thou destroyest all their memory." - Young's Literal Translation

Notice in the Latin the word *gigantes* (earthborn) appears, which is the same exact word the Greeks use, and is where we get the English word giant. In the Douay-Rheims Bible, the word "giants" is there. Finally in the Young's Literal Translation, the word is Rephaim (shades, ghosts, the dead ones), which was one of the tribes of the Nephilim. The King James Version is not completely clear in its translation of the passage so it is important to point out the other translations that include the reference to the giants not being resurrected.

Vampirism and The Bible

Contrary to popular belief the vampire legend did not start in modern times. The modern vampire has taken on several changes from the old legends, but the story originates in Babylon. Much of the reason for a misunderstanding of a vampire is due to the commercialization of the subject. Blood drinking was a big deal in ancient times because blood was believed to be the source of life.

> "But flesh with the life thereof, which is the blood thereof, shall ye not eat." – Genesis 9:4

As soon as Noah got off of the ark God established a law forbidding them from consuming blood. Was God warning Noah in advance or creating this law based on previous events? If the stories of the Nephilim devouring flesh and drinking blood are true, then it may have been based on events preceding the flood. When Moses comes into the picture, God once again expresses the need to avoid the consumption of blood.

> "For it is the life of all flesh; the blood of it is for the life thereof: therefore I said unto the children of Israel, Ye shall eat the blood of no manner of flesh: for the life of all flesh is the blood thereof: whosoever eateth it shall be cut off." – Leviticus 17:14

God was very serious about not consuming blood. In my opinion it had to be somewhat of a major issue for God to bring it up as soon as Noah left the ark, and then again as soon as the Hebrews left Egypt. Once again, the violation of the temple (body) seems to be the objective, and it may be why we find blood drinkers all through the pages of human history.

Science Fact vs. Science Fiction

Science and our government like to "test the water" before releasing any major information. The Island of Dr. Moreau (H.G. Wells) was written in 1896, and a first movie was adapted from the book in 1977. The premise of the movie was a doctor combining human and animal DNA to produce hybrid creatures. In 1993 Jurassic Park sparked public interest in cloning and DNA manipulation. In 1996 The Island of Dr. Moreau was remade and Jurassic Park debuted on network television, followed by the story of Dolly (sheep), the first mammal to be cloned using nuclear transfer. Now that we have compiled the information, we need to figure out how all of these events are linked. According to the cycle of recorded history, beings from the sky appear to man just before major advances in technology are made. There are several cultures that testify to this cycle.

- Sumer
- Egypt
- Greece
- Mayan
- Inca
- Aztec
- Maori

This sudden burst of technology in combination with reports of beings from other worlds visiting earth lends credibility to the claims of these cultures. These were the same cultures that believed human and animal DNA could be combined to create new and fascinating creatures called hybrids or chimeras. The concept of a chimera is a human with animal characteristics or animal with human characteristics. There are those Christians that write many of these facts off as mythology simply because they have been told to do so. Personal belief does not equate to factual information. Because many people in church have been brainwashed into dismissing everything because "it's not in the Bible", they will be in a very dangerous spiritual position of trying to reconcile the lies they have been taught, with the reality that is staring them in the face.

Doorways To Demonic Activity

Spiritual doorways refer to actions or activities that make someone more susceptible to negative spiritual activity. Once opened, these doorways can lead to demonic infestation and even possession of the individual. These doorways can be opened on purpose or by accident. Those most in danger of opening a doorway are those that do not know or believe that they exist. When studying the supernatural, we find the common thread of entities requesting an invitation in order to present themselves to the intended victim. This request for an invitation is most prevalent in the vampire legend and even in some alien abduction reports. If something asks for an invitation, do not give it because it is trying to get you to open a spiritual doorway that will allow it to come and go as it pleases.

Possible Doorways

- **Hypnotism:** Allowing yourself to be placed in a vulnerable state where you release conscious control can open up doorways unintentionally.

- **Yoga:** This ancient practice is presented as a means of relaxation, but is very stressful on the body. Performing certain moves wrong can lead to such extremes as death. The goal of Yoga is to eliminate the soul from the wheel of reincarnation and become one with Brahma, or in other words, the ultimate goal is physical death.

- **Ouija Board:** This is a means of opening a door on purpose. The Spirit Board links back to at least 1100 B.C. China. The goal is to make contact with the spirit world. Opening this door is definitely not suggested.

- **Séance:** Talking directly with the dead is a practice that was forbidden in the Old Testament. On one occasion the Witch of Endor created a line of communication with the dead for king Saul, but Samuel was not the only thing she conjured up. Fallen angels were seen coming out of the ground.

It is important that we avoid dabbling into these different practices no matter how innocent they may seem. Evil is most effective when it does not appear to be evil.

Demonic Possession

Demons seem to have the need to possess and control people or animals in order to manifest their presence, as seen in the story of the Gaderenes (Luke 8:26-33). Another terrifying aspect of demons is that many of them can inhabit the same space (Mark 5:9). A common misinterpretation is that there were 1,000 demons inside of the man that was possessed by Legion, but a Roman legion could consist of as many as 4,200 soldiers. Possessed individuals seem to display enhanced or superhuman abilities such as, super strength (Mark 5:4) and immunity to fire (Matthew 17:15). In movies such as The Exorcist, demons display an ability to move objects without touching them and speak in multiple voices simultaneously. Many people claim that demonic possession was just an ancient way of diagnosing mental problems, however Matthew 4:24 makes it clear that they understood the difference between demonic possession and mental problems. Mental illness also does not explain super strength or immunity to fire. There also seems to be different levels of demons that were immune to the disciples' attempts at exorcism (Matthew 17:18-21). Demons are also very dangerous and on at least one occasion a single demon beat and humiliated seven men (Acts 19:13-16) for trying to cast him out without the proper authority. Demon possession is real and it still happens.

The History of Exorcism

There is a lot of mystery that surrounds the ancient practice of performing an exorcism. Hollywood movies have commercialized the practice until it is no longer believed by many people. While many people in the modern age do not believe in spirits that possess human bodies, it was a widely held belief in the ancient world. There were also many ways that these cultures believed an exorcism could be performed.

Chapter 7: The Origin of Demons

- Name of Jesus
- Exorcism
- *Blessed Oil
- *Holy Water
- *Crucifix
- Music
- Fasting
- Prayer

Much of what we know about exorcism comes from Catholic based movies, which usually consist of long exorcism rituals which were not conducted in the Bible. Crucifixes, Blessed Oil, and Holy Water may not be effective against demons in a real life situation, but it sure looks convincing in the movies. However, rebuking in the name of Jesus, fasting, and prayer are known to work if the one doing the casting out is saved. The unsaved may find themselves in the same position as the seven sons of Sceva (Acts 19:16). Exorcism has been part of the human existence since shortly after Noah's flood. Throughout history, music has been the traditional way of appeasing and driving away unwanted spirits. The first account of this in the Bible is when David plays music for Saul in 1 Samuel 16:23.

> "And it came to pass, when the evil spirit from God was upon Saul, that David took an harp, and played with his hand: so Saul was refreshed, and was well, and the evil spirit departed from him." - 1 Samuel 16:23

The oldest known references to rebuking in the name of the Lord is found in Zechariah 3:2 and Jude 1:9, both in direct reference to opposing Satan. When Jesus comes on the scene He commands demons to come out of people with authority and gives His disciples the authority to cast them out in His name (Luke 10:17). After one occasion of the disciples returning from an unsuccessful exorcism, He reveals that certain kinds of exorcisms require fasting and prayer (Mark 9:29). Unfortunately, the Bible does not give us the details as to what kind of spirits are immune to obeying the name of Jesus and why it is necessary to engage in heavier spiritual warfare with them through fasting and prayer. That fact alone should make us open our eyes and take spiritual warfare very seriously.

The Breakdown

Both the Bible and mythology from around the world tell us that there is a very strong connection between the creation of hybrid creatures and demonic manifestations. It is nothing more than modern human arrogance to assume that we are the first group of people to experiment with hybridization, especially when hybrids line the pages of almost every ancient text in existence. The direction in which science is moving seems to be spiritually influenced and aimed toward the goal of corrupting all flesh once again, as it was in the days of Noah.

Chapter in Review

- Do angels and demons have different names?
- Do demons have a connection to hybridization?
- What were the Shed?
- What were the Sa'iyr?
- What were the Nephilim?
- What are germ line parahumans?
- What are somatic parahumans?

Critical Thinking

- Could modern hybrids turn into demons when they die?
- Did hybrid animals exist in the past?
- Are genetics being used as a means of spiritual warfare?
- Do somatic parahumans exist now?
- Should we accept a shot that would make us somatic parahumans?

The Plan of Salvation

The plan of salvation is not difficult or complicated at all. In fact it can be summed up in one single verse. All you need to do in order to be saved is the following:

Chapter 7: The Origin of Demons

> That if thou shalt confess with thy mouth the Lord Jesus, and shalt believe in thine heart that God hath raised him from the dead, thou shalt be saved." - Romans 10:9

If you have accepted Christ, your next step should be to get your hands on a King James Version of the Bible. Before joining any church, you should have a good foundation in scripture without the influences of any teacher. Once you have a general understanding of scripture, visit a few churches before deciding on a church home. Make sure you check behind the pastor and do not just accept their word for anything without checking (Acts 17:11). If asking questions is discouraged, steer clear of that church at all costs.

Key Scriptures For Review

- Genesis 6
- Leviticus 16
- Leviticus 17
- Deuteronomy 32
- 1 Samuel 16
- 1 Kings 11
- Job 4
- Psalms 106
- Ecclesiastes 1
- Isaiah 13
- Daniel 2
- Mark 3
- Matthew 10
- Matthew 24
- 1 Corinthians 3
- 1 Corinthians 6
- 2 Corinthians 5
- 2 Peter 1
- Jude 1
- Revelation 9

Submit Your Questions

If you have more questions about spiritual warfare, angels, demons, the supernatural, or the Bible in general, you are welcome to submit your questions to me personally. Answers to your questions will be posted as an article on the website for everyone to see.

www.MinisterFortson.com

Angels 103: The History of Angels

Chapter 8: The Technology of Angels

> "There is no neutral ground in the universe; every square inch, every split second, is claimed by God and counter-claimed by Satan" - C.S. Lewis

A major part of the success of any society is the development of their technology. In modern times, much of our technology is freely shared among nations, with the exception of technology crucial to national security. As we trace the development of technology throughout history, we find that there are many stories in which some of these technological developments did not originate here on Earth.

Do Angels Have Access To Technology?

In order to establish the theory that angels may be responsible for at least influencing human technology, we first need to establish whether or not the Bible makes any such connection. In this field of study, there are some very wild theories that tend to fly around and it is very easy to fall into that trap if the Bible is not used as our blueprint to inspire research. When we stick to the pages of the Bible, what we find is one of the first signs of a technologically aware civilization.

> "Though I speak with the tongues of men and of angels, and have not charity, I am become as sounding brass, or a tinkling cymbal." - 1 Corinthians 13:31

Communication is the key to developing a successful society and technology. Based on the above verse we know that angels indeed have their own language, which is distinctly different than human language, according to Paul. There are many that believe the language of angels is a slight variation of the Hebrew alphabet. This belief has been around for a very long time and is featured in many popular movies such as The Prophecy series. Many of us do not immediately recognize this language that is referred to as "angelic script" or "*Malachim*" because we are not familiar with the alphabet that has been associated with them. Since languages are often made up in movies, many of us may assume that the strange markings were made up by the movie producers for effect. The fact is that many of these strange markings come from ancient sources and ancient beliefs that revolve around a period when angels and gods were believed to have interacted with mankind.

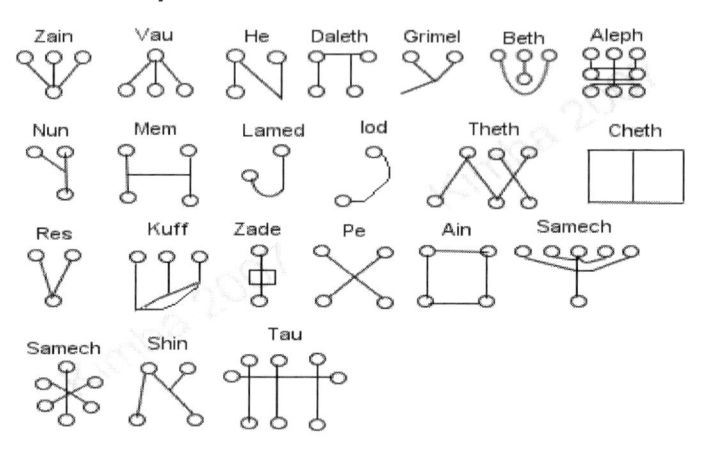

Alphabet "Malachim"

Zain	Vau	He	Daleth	Grimel	Beth	Aleph
Nun	Mem	Lamed	Iod	Theth		Cheth
Res	Kuff	Zade	Pe	Ain	Samech	
Samech	Shin	Tau				

If the names for the letters are not familiar to you, it is because you have not familiarized yourself with the Hebrew Alphabet. The chart below shows the names of the Hebrew Alphabet. Compare the names in the chart below with the chart above.

The Hebrew Alphabet

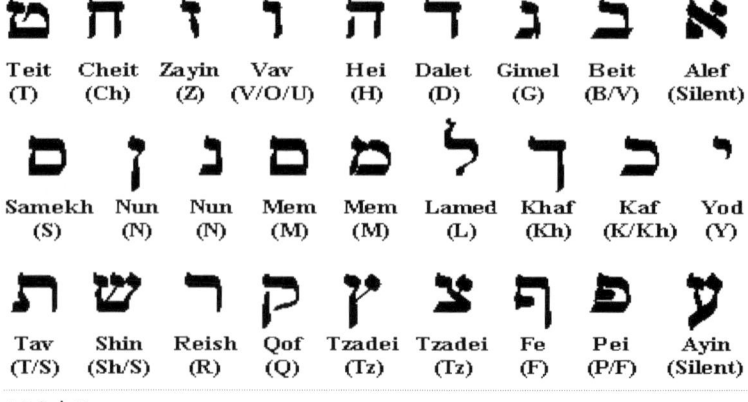

ט	ח	ז	ו	ה	ד	ג	ב	א
Teit (T)	Cheit (Ch)	Zayin (Z)	Vav (V/O/U)	Hei (H)	Dalet (D)	Gimel (G)	Beit (B/V)	Alef (Silent)

ס	ן	נ	ם	מ	ל	ך	כ	י
Samekh (S)	Nun (N)	Nun (N)	Mem (M)	Mem (M)	Lamed (L)	Khaf (Kh)	Kaf (K/Kh)	Yod (Y)

ת	ש	ר	ק	ץ	צ	ף	פ	ע
Tav (T/S)	Shin (Sh/S)	Reish (R)	Qof (Q)	Tzadei (Tz)	Tzadei (Tz)	Fe (F)	Pei (P/F)	Ayin (Silent)

While we cannot be sure that the *Malachim* language is indeed the language of angels, the Bible does confirm that an angelic language does exist. The Biblical reference to angelic language is just the beginning. There are several more references in the Bible to angels having access to technology far beyond what was humanly possible at the time. The next Biblical evidence we will look at is the *merkabah*.

Chariots of The Gods

Throughout the Bible we find angels traveling in what the Hebrews referred to as *merkabah* and *rekeb*. When the translators of the King James Bible came across the word, they interpreted it to mean "chariot", and it appears as such in the Bible. However, the word is far more complex than the KJV translation conveys.

The *merkabah* is a huge anomaly and largely passed over because of its interpretation as simply being a chariot. The word *merkabah* is not a chariot in the sense of having four wheels, but is a more general word that means "vehicle". In Jewish Mysticism and other teachings on the metaphysical, the *merkabah* is a vehicle that allows transport between our physical reality and the spiritual plane. Normally we would completely ignore mysticism and metaphysical teachings, but in this case there seems to be a little bit of truth to these beliefs. In the Bible we find the following in reference to the *merkabah*.

> "For, behold, the LORD will come with fire, and with his chariots (merkabah) like a whirlwind, to render his anger with fury, and his rebuke with flames of fire." - Isaiah 66:15

Is God coming to carry out His wrath and anger in a wooden wagon with four wheels drawn by horses? That is highly unlikely. Notice that the scripture clearly describes the merkabah as being "like a whirlwind." In this case there are actually quite a few descriptions of these vehicles in the Bible.

> "And I looked, and, behold, a whirlwind came out of the north, a great cloud, and a fire infolding itself, and a bright-

> ness was about it, and out of the midst thereof as the colour of amber, out of the midst of the fire. Also out of the midst thereof came the likeness of four living creatures. And this was their appearance; they had the likeness of a man." - Ezekiel 1:4-5

Here in Ezekiel we find the arrival of God and another reference to this whirlwind. If we read the verse carefully we notice that there are four creatures that come "out of the midst" of this whirlwind. These living creatures were not men, but had the likeness of men. We usually refer to these four living creatures as *cherubim,* which is one of the ranks of angels. Many Ancient Astronaut theorists actually cite this arrival as proof of extraterrestrials in the Bible. However, their explanation may be sugar coating something more sinister and Satanic than they imagine. The following is a more traditional depiction of what the *merkabah* are believed look like.

Chapter 8: The Technology of Angels

While the arrival of the *merkabah* is usually associated with God, the There are a few other verses which describe the angels showing up without God, in a vehicle called the *rekeb*. The *rekeb* have a little more detail associated with them than the *merkabah*, and the details surrounding his vehicle are even stranger in retrospect to what was humanly possible during this period of time.

> "And it came to pass, as they still went on, and talked, that, behold, there appeared a chariot of fire, and horses of fire, and parted them both asunder; and Elijah went up by a whirlwind into heaven." - 2 Kings 2:11

The association of the *rekeb* with the commonly depicted chariot is because of the use of the word "horse" in the verse. The term "horse" used in this verse is the Hebrew word *cuwc*. This word is actually more of a description of an action than it is a reference to a specific animal. This same word actually has three different meanings depending on the circumstance and context of the story in which it is used:

- To skip for joy.
- Leap like a horse.
- Fly swiftly like a swallow.

If we read 2 Kings again in context, it becomes easier to narrow down the most likely description of what happened. We know that this vehicle came out of the sky so it is likely that the reference to swift flight would be more accurate. The text seems to be pointing to the arrival of a flaming vehicle that moved swiftly through the air like a swallow. Unlike Christ, who is omnipresent, angels seem to have to travel the distance from point A to point B. One such example is found in Daniel Chapter 10:

> "Then said he unto me, Fear not, Daniel: for from the first day that thou didst set thine heart to understand, and to chasten thyself before thy God, thy words were heard, and I am come for thy words. But the prince of the kingdom of Persia withstood me one and twenty days: but, lo, Michael, one of the chief princes, came to help me; and I remained there with the kings of Persia." - Daniel 10:12-13

Angels may be able to change from spiritual to physical instantly, but it seems they may actually be required to travel to their intended location. The angel that was sent to Daniel claims that he was sent out the very first day that Daniel began his fast, but he was intercepted by the "prince of the kingdom of Persia". This other being held up the angel's travel for twenty one days. If angels could simply teleport to their intended location, he probably would not have been held up.

As our understanding of technology and the world advances, there are certain things in the Bible that become clearer. During the time of the KJV's translation, people had no frame of reference for swiftly flying, flaming, vehicles. The only vehicle transportation that existed were chariots and boats. In the modern age we now have swiftly flying vehicles that shoot out flames. According to the Mayans, Sumerians, and various other cultures, beings from the sky brought them their advanced knowledge of the universe. They spoke about things in their texts that we are just now beginning to understand. Secular researchers have actually started looking at strange verses like these and tying them to what is known as the Ancient Astronaut Theory.

The Ancient Alien Deception

In a nutshell, the Ancient Astronaut theory teaches that our world was visited by highly advanced alien beings from another planet. There are a few disturbing ideas associated with this new take on Intelligent Design. These ideas completely attack and redefine the Bible, but more importantly how we view Christ. There is a systematic process involved in getting people to accept this false view, which requires someone to completely renounce their prior religious beliefs very slowly.

Tactic #1: The entire Ancient Astronaut theory has religious implications. This is not just an issue of whether or not God is an alien, but a debate of whether or not God is who He claims to be. The first step is to get people to question the reliability of the Bible, which is God's word. By questioning His word, you are questioning Him from which the word proceeded.

Chapter 8: The Technology of Angels

Tactic #2: The next step is to completely replace God with a combination of pantheism and modern evolution. The Ancient Astronaut theorists believed that E.T. evolved somewhere else in the universe and eventually created us. According to them, we mistook these creators as God/gods/angels, but they are our true creators.

Tactic #3: Now that God has been replaced with E.T., it's time to upgrade Lucifer as the savior and downplay Christ as nothing more than an ascended alien master. There are many groups that believe E.T is the creator of mankind, and these groups teach that Lucifer only wanted to enlighten mankind when he tempted Eve in the garden. In their version of events, he is viewed as a savior and advocate of mankind. On the other side of the coin, Christ is downgraded from being the son of God to being nothing more than the son of a god. The tactic here is subtle because it draws in those people that do not believe in the devil, and retains those that do by presenting him as an alien instead of presenting him as a supernatural being. Christians that are not founded in the word are drawn in because accepting this belief does not mean they have to deny the existence of Christ, His miracles, or resurrection, but they just have to accept a naturalistic explanation of those events. This new explanation completely negates His true identity and the intended purpose of His death which is the salvation of mankind.

Tactic #4: The Rapture of the Church is explained away as a cleansing of antiquated theology which is holding back the next evolution of human kind. This explanation has a tendency to target only the religions that trace their origin to Abraham:

- Judaism
- Christianity
- Islam

There seems to be a very practical reason for targeting these three belief systems. In the Bible very specific promises were made to Jacob, Ishmael, and the Church. These three religions all claim to worship the God of the Bible, we all believe in fallen angels and Satan as an evil being, and none of us are willing to incorporate a naturalistic view into our belief system. While it is not something that is talked about much in public, Islam does profess a belief in UFOs and their supernatural origin. If Christians are Raptured at some point, they still have to worry about the Jews and Muslims. By targeting people that are holding on to their beliefs instead of accepting this new ideology, it will eventually lead to hate, violence, and the possible final attempted extermination of the Semitic people. This belief in a religious cleansing is probably more dangerous than many people realize.

Tactic #5: The revealing of an alien presence is the hope and dream of many people in this day and age. Many believe that this will be the final nail in the coffin of religion because there is nothing more convincing than powerful beings that can be seen, smelled, and touched, all while claiming to be our creators. In this field of study, there are some, including myself that believe the Antichrist will have some association with this "alien" revelation. The Bible mentions a deception so powerful that it could potentially deceive the very elect, if it was possible (Matthew 24:4).

Opinion: I believe the "very elect" may not refer to all Christians, but to an even smaller group within Christianity, usually referred to as "the remnant" in scripture. This smaller group will likely consist of people that are informed about the subject, waiting for these events to occur, and are still somewhat impressed by what they are seeing. Although impressed, they will not fall for the deception and abandon their faith. The rest of the world will be deceived into believing that these *merkabah* are piloted by alien beings instead of fallen angels.

All of the pieces have been put in place and all that is left to do is for Satan and his fallen angles to make an appearance and claim to be E.T. This is another area where some Ancient Astronaut believers differ from what the Bible says. While we are waiting for the return of Christ, they are waiting for the return of Lucifer. While this in no way reflects the beliefs of the majority of Ancient Astronaut Theorists, there are a very small number that believe Jesus and Satan will have a final battle (Armageddon) in which Lucifer emerges victorious.

If the course of history leads to an "alien" revelation, there are many Christian scholars that believe it will give rise to the

Chapter 8: The Technology of Angels

Antichrist and the one world government. The Antichrist's relationship with these fallen angels may allow him to easily usher in an age of peace that allows him to assume control of the entire world, which will lead to the next tactic.

Tactic #6: The Mark of The Beast is found in Revelation 13. It is the Antichrist that demands people to receive the mark or they will not be able to buy or sell anything. In Chapter 7 we discussed transhumansim, hybridization, and how it all relates to the Bible. The culmination of this plan may be something that could have only been conceived by one of the fallen angels.

Usurping Salvation

Until we start putting the pieces of the puzzle together, it is sometimes hard to see how the days of Noah, fallen angels, UFOs, alien abduction, transhumanism, and hybridization can all be linked to a common goal. The entire goal seems to be to usurp salvation itself.

> **Usurp** (verb) – "to seize and hold (a position, office, power, etc.) by force or without legal right:"[1]

One of the dangers of not learning about the spiritual implications of hybridization and transhumanism is that it does not seem to be as spiritually dangerous as it really is. When Satan entered the garden, he could not force Eve to eat the forbidden fruit. He had to convince her to make the decision herself and rebel against God's law. Here we are again, at the peak of human history, and we are once again being tempted to taste a forbidden fruit.

Theory: The research into creating Somatic Parahumans may be used by the Antichrist in order to physically change human DNA. This change would turn them into animal/human hybrids, thus making them exempt from accepting a fully human Savior.

---

[1] http://dictionary.reference.com/browse/usurp

This theory may make many people feel very uneasy and it should because it is the perfect way to insure that as many people as possible share the Lake of Fire with Satan. The following verse has been interpreted many ways throughout history, but it may point to something much bigger in scope than it is usually given credit for:

> "And except those days should be shortened, there should no flesh be saved: but for the elect's sake those days shall be shortened." – Matthew 24:22

If you can think of a way to wipe out all life on the planet, it has probably been applied as an interpretation to this verse. Many believe that at some point it will become so bad that it threatens to wipe out flesh on the planet, but that may not be the case. In Noah's time all flesh had become genetically "corrupted", with the exception of eight people. Why should this time be any different at all?

> "And the third angel followed them, saying with a loud voice, If any man worship the beast and his image, and receive his mark in his forehead, or in his hand, The same shall drink of the wine of the wrath of God, which is poured out without mixture into the cup of his indignation; and he shall be tormented with fire and brimstone in the presence of the holy angels, and in the presence of the Lamb:" – Revelation 14:9-10

Whatever the Mark of The Beast turns out to be, and however it is implemented, accepting it is literally going past the point of no return. It is entirely possible that this whole process will be jumpstarted by the arrival of fallen angels in what will be perceived as UFOs.

The Ancient Builders

All over the world archaeologists are discovering structures that defy the technology and perceived know how of the time period. The commonly accepted explanations of thousands of workers using ramps and pulleys seem absurd once we begin digging into just how megalithic some of these structures were.

Chapter 8: The Technology of Angels

Modern man, as recent as the last twenty years, became capable of moving some of these stone blocks. What we find when we dig into the history, myths, and legends surrounding some of these sites, is that they tell us a completely different story than the mainstream media would like us to believe.

Gobekli Tepe

Gobekli Tepe is believed to be almost 12,000 years old, and pre-dates any civilization found on earth by several thousand years. When found, it appeared to be deliberately buried in sand, for reasons unknown.[2] Göbekli Tepe is the oldest human-made structure yet discovered.[3] The site is located on a hilltop, and contains 20 round, subterranean structures. Each building has a diameter of 10-30 meters, and is decorated with massive T-shaped limestone pillars. Each pillar is around eight feet tall, and weighs up to seven tons. The limestone slabs were quarried from bedrock pits located around 100 meters from the hilltop, with neolithic workers presumably using flint tools to carve the bedrock. However, no tools have been found at the site or the quarry.

---

[2] History Channel
[3] "The World's First Temple". *Archaeology magazine*. Nov/Dec 2008. p. 23.

The Ruins of Baalbek

Baalbek is probably one of the most massive sites on the planet. It consisted of three temples dedicated to the worship of Venus, Bacchus, and Jupiter. Here are a few quick facts about Baalbek:

- The walls are built with 24 stones, each weighing approximately 300 tons.
- The largest retaining wall consists of 3 stones, each weighing approximately 750 tons.[4]
- The stone of the pregnant woman weighs an estimated 1,069 tons.
- The largest stone weighs approximately 1,322 tons.

As we can see from the numbers, this structure is massive to say the least. The prevailing theory is that Roman cranes were used to build Baalbek, but that also does not appear to be very logical. The current estimation is that each Roman crane could lift about 7.5 tons.[5]

---

[4] Martin Isler, Sticks, Stones and Shadows University of Oklahoma Press, December 31, 2001

[5] Lancaster, Lynne (1999), "Building Trajan's Column", *American Journal of Archaeology* **103** (3): 419-439

Chapter 8: The Technology of Angels

If we examine the picture, we notice a tiny black speck near the second to last column on the left. That is a man wearing a white shirt and black pants. We can clearly see that Baalbek exceeds the technology that was available at the time, but we are expected to believe that ancient man built this monument with primitive cranes and pulleys.

Stonehenge

Traditionally, Stonehenge is believed to have been created by the Druids. The Druids were a group of Celtic priests that were believed to have participated in human sacrifices. The connection between Druids and human sacrifice is established in the writing of no less than four historical people:

1. Lucan
2. Julius Caesar
3. Suetonius
4. Cicero

Diodorus Siculus believed that the Druids were making sacrifices to Teutates (Celtic god of tribes), Esus (Gaulish god of the woods), and Taranis (Celtic god of thunder).

> "These men predict the future by observing the flight and calls of birds and by the sacrifice of holy animals: all orders of society are in their power... and in very important matters they prepare a human victim, plunging a dagger into his chest; by observing the way his limbs convulse as he falls and the gushing of his blood, they are able to read the future." - Diodorus Siculus

Many believe that these ritual sacrifices took place at Stonehenge which is also believed to be a huge celestial calendar. While we do not know exactly what Stonehenge was used for, its connection with human sacrifice points us toward the ancient practice of summoning the gods.

There is no shortage to the list of megalithic structures that appear around the world. Science has made many unfounded claims and many unsuccessful attempts to prove how these structures were built in the past. Because of this, many people have started to go back and reconsider the ancient stories of the gods passing down knowledge and technology to mankind, which enabled them to accomplish tasks that seem impossible

Chapter 8: The Technology of Angels

for the time period and level of technology. One result of this interaction between mankind and the gods is believed to be ancient man's knowledge of the stars.

The Martian Monuments

In 1976, an area of Mars known as Cydonia was photographed and what appeared there was what many believe to be a monument that resembles a face. While the anomaly itself is the subject of much debate, it has never been debunked scientifically. There are some that believe it is the work of a lost civilization that once inhabited mars, and others believe that it is left over proof from an angelic civilization that inhabited the universe prior to the events in Genesis 1:2.

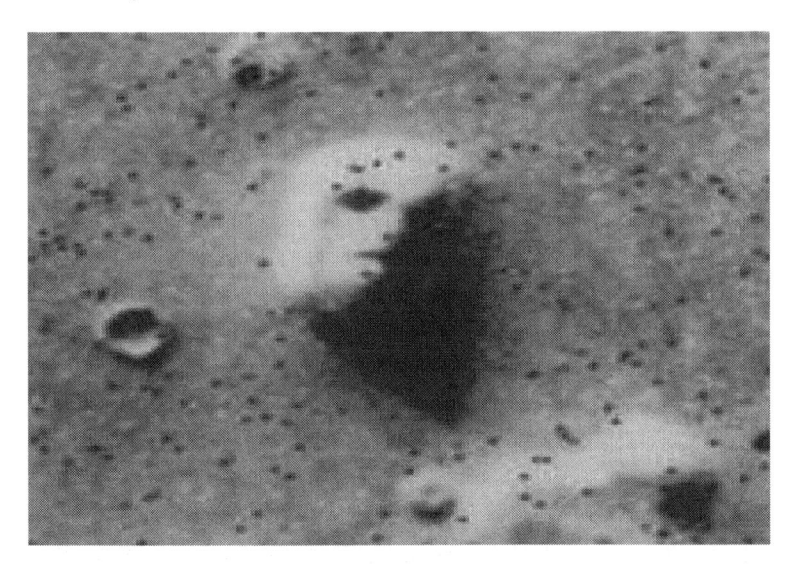

In addition to the above highly controversial picture, there are other structures that appear on mars that many believe resemble the design of Old Testament altars and Egyptian pyramids. These structures could simply be landscape anomalies or they could be part of a bigger deception.

The Ancient Calendars

All over the world we find calendars that display an uncanny accuracy and far exceed the knowledge believed to have been available to ancient civilizations. The following calendars are just a few examples:

- Mayan Calendar (South America)
- Phoenix Calendar (Africa)
- Kali Yuga (India)

The above list is best known because of the date at which all of them point to as a major transformation for mankind and the return of the "gods" of mythology. That date is 2012, and it has been highly commercialized by the media to the point that it no longer resembles what is actually reflected in these calendars. The subject of 2012 is discussed in detail in my book, As The Days of Noah Were.

Chapter 8: The Technology of Angels

One very interesting culture is the Dogon tribe of Mali because of how primitive they were, their knowledge of the stars, and how they came to possess this knowledge. According to the Dogon, fishlike gods called the Nommo brought them knowledge about the stars. It is important to point out that like most beliefs, even though the Nommo were considered to be gods, they had a creator (Amma) and were not all powerful. According to the Dogon, the Nommo gave them extensive knowledge about the Sirius star system, which was not confirmed until the mid 1800s. The simple fact is that this knowledge of the stars had to come from somewhere and the Dogon testimony is the exact same testimony that we find in the book of Enoch, Greece, Rome, Hopi, India, China, Russia, Norse, Celtic, and other diverse cultures from around the world.

From a Biblical perspective, there are only two other groups that could have access to this type of knowledge: God and the angels. According to all of the ancient accounts it was the created gods that came down and passed along this information. These were likely fallen angels interfering in the affairs of mankind in order to set the stage for a much bigger deception that we will discuss in the next chapter.

Human Sacrifice & Forbidden Knowledge

In ancient times, it was believed that one of the ways to summon information from the gods or to get the gods themselves to appear was by spilling human blood. We find this practice in the Bible and in other cultures as well.

- Ammon
- Moab
- Mayan
- Babylon
- Aztec
- Greece

This practice continued on throughout history into one of the most widely known atrocities to ever happen. Many people are familiar with WWII, Hitler, and the Holocaust, but not many people realize what was going on was spiritual in nature. The Nazis were very much into occult magic and UFOs. In fact, Project Paperclip is a now very well known attempt by the Nazis to develop what we would call a UFO. The picture below is believed to be from released Nazi documents of a top secret craft known as Haunebu II.

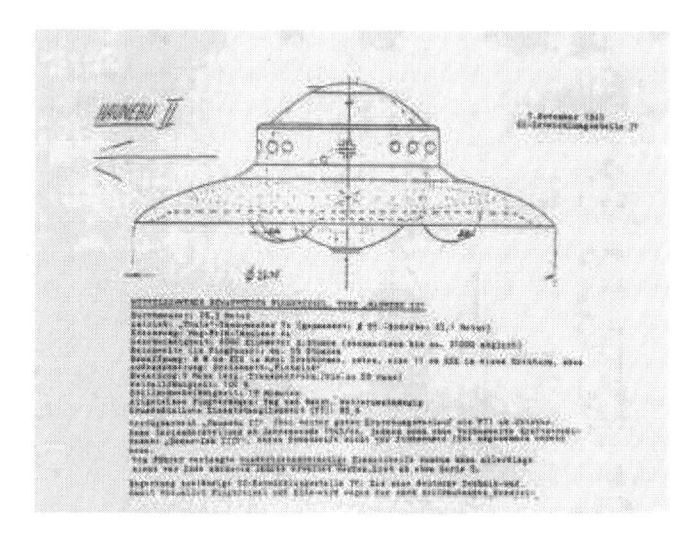

This craft was just the tip of the iceberg when it came to the Nazis. Rumor has it that they were attempting to open a portal into the spirit realm, which is depicted in the opening scenes of the movie Hellboy. Perhaps the most widely known belief of Hitler was the arrival of a master race he called the 4th Reich. This is widely taught in schools, but what is not taught is that he believed this was a race of ancient god/men hybrids that would return some day. Hitler's goal was to expedite their return through mass human sacrifice, which is what the Holocaust was. Hitler officially began his extermination camps in July 1942. These were different than the concentration and forced labor camps in that people were being placed in huge ovens and burned alive. This practice was much like the one God condemned in the Old Testament worship of Molech.[6]

---

[6] Harran, Marilyn (2000). *The Holocaust Chronicles, A History in Words and Pictures*. Publications International. p. Pg.321.

Chapter 8: The Technology of Angels

In November 1944 strange craft suddenly appeared all over the place. The Nazis thought they belonged to the Americans and the Americans thought they belonged to the opposing side. Michael D. Swords said the following:

> "During WWII, the foo fighter experiences of [Allied] pilots were taken very seriously. Accounts of these cases were presented to heavyweight scientists, such as David Griggs, Luis Alvarez and H.P. Robertson. The phenomenon was never explained. Most of the information about the issue has never been released by military intelligence."[7]

According to some of the pilots, these Foo Fighters were fast moving, round, glowing balls of light that followed their fighters over Germany. Some of the fighters reported being toyed with by these balls of light and afterward that lights would simply vanish. These are not the reports of civilians on the ground seeing strange military lights. These reports came from trained Air Force pilots that knew something out of the ordinary was happening. What they may have encountered were the *merkabah* being guided by fallen angels.

The Legacy of Human Sacrifice

How do you get people to voluntarily sacrifice their children in a modern world? You rewrap the old concept of Eugenics as Planned Parenthood. Margaret Sanger, the founder of Planned Parenthood, held many of Hitler's beliefs, including a belief in Eugenics. Eugenics is the belief that only the smartest, wealthiest, and genetically pure people should be allowed to reproduce. The belief also teaches that the poor and genetically imperfect should be sterilized or encouraged to abort their unborn children. Andrew Hoffman wrote a very thorough book on Eugenics and how it ties in to the end time scenario and spiritual deception. His book is called, <u>The NWO and The Eugenics</u>

---

[7] Swords, Michael D. "Ufology: What Have We Learned?" *Journal of Scientific Exploration*, Vol 20, No 4, pp. 545-589, 2006

Wars. It is highly recommended for anyone that wants to know what Eugenics is all about.

When Hitler's ovens started sacrificing millions of Jews, the Foo Fighters showed up in mass shortly after. In our modern times UFO sightings are on the rise and the number of abortions worldwide are estimated to be 42 million per year.[8] To put this in perspective, there are an estimated 205 million pregnancies per year. Roughly 1/5 of those children are being exterminated before birth. The fetuses that are not used in stem cell research are then incinerated by medical professionals. This practice of burning children ties directly back to the Old Testament.

> "And they caused their sons and their daughters to pass through the fire, and used divination and enchantments, and sold themselves to do evil in the sight of the LORD, to provoke him to anger." - 2 Kings 17:17

There are many people that recognize this practice for exactly what it is. The scientific response was to redefine what it means to be alive so that people would not view abortion as murder. Hitler sacrificed roughly 6,000,000 people during a period of three years, not counting the ones that died from the concentration camp conditions. If his sacrifice of nearly 6,000,000 people heralded the arrival of the Foo Fighters, is it a coincidence that we currently kill 42,000,000 unborn children per year and UFO sightings have increased since the 1940s? In the Old Testament, this same practice of child sacrifice was addressed in the book of Psalms.

> "Yea, they sacrificed their sons and their daughters unto devils, And shed innocent blood, even the blood of their sons and of their daughters, whom they sacrificed unto the idols of Canaan: and the land was polluted with blood. Thus were they defiled with their own works, and went a whoring with their own inventions. Therefore was the wrath of the LORD

---

[8] Shah, I.; Ahman, E. (December 2009). "Unsafe abortion: global and regional incidence, trends, consequences, and challenges". *Journal of Obstetrics and Gynaecology Canada* **31** (12): 1149-58.

> kindled against his people, insomuch that he abhorred his own inheritance." - Psalm 106:37-40

The abortion issue in America is not just a right vs. left or a right vs. wrong issue, it is an issue of continuing pagan rituals designed to worship demons and provoke God to anger. It was also through these human sacrifices that many cultures claim to have obtained various aspects of their knowledge and technology.

Heavenly Beings and Human Technology

According to the Greeks, Prometheus was a very intelligent and deceptive god (titan). Against the will of Zeus (the supreme god of the Greeks), he stole fire and gave it to men. Because he did this, mankind learned war and as a punishment Zeus chained him to a mountain where a giant eagle would eat his liver everyday. Although the story of Prometheus is very well known to those that study Greek mythology, there are other stories from around the world that suggest at some point, a celestial being gave men fire in violation of a divine command. Here are just a few of the cultures from around the world that speak of beings giving the technology of fire making to man:

- Georgian Mythology - Amirani
- Rig Veda - Matarisvan
- Cherokee Myth - Grandmother Spider
- Creek Indians - Rabbit
- Polynesians - Maui
- Book of Enoch - Fallen angels and Azazel

If we look at the last example, the book of Enoch pops up again. This time the event is credited to fallen angels, and one specifically by the name of Azazel. The Book of Enoch also says that these angels taught men how to use tools, perform sorcery, and make weapons. That is another technology that men did not have at the time, according to the Book of Enoch. Also notice that instead of calling them gods, the writer of the Book of Enoch is referring to them as fallen angels. A recurring theme throughout the book is different groups of people talking about similar events, but interpreting what these beings are based on what they believe.

We will begin our dissection of the Prometheus story by looking at his name. In both Greek and Hebrew, names meant something and described the character of the person. Prometheus means "forethought", which would suggest that he was a planner. His disobedience was a planned event, but was it for the purpose of bettering mankind or getting mankind to destroy itself? The underlying theme to these stories represents a huge leap in technology. The gods/angels had the technology to master fire, and according the myths and legends, humans did not. They shared their technology with mankind, which resulted in a more destructive behavior. Advanced beings giving mankind technology that is way beyond their understanding is a recurring theme in Sci-Fi series and movies, and it usually leads to some catastrophe on earth. The majority of modern day Sci-Fi concepts can be found by simply learning what ancient cultures believed. Another clue to the technology associated with Prometheus can be found in our own modern culture. Here are just a few of the clubs, organizations, and businesses that are associated with the name Prometheus.

- Prometheus Society – High IQ Society 600 times more selective than Mensa.
- Prometea – A cloned horse born May 28, 2003. The name comes from Prometheus.
- Prometheus Books – A company that publishes scientific, educational, and popular books.
- Prometheus Therapeutics and Diagnostics – A professional pharmaceutical company located in San Diego, CA.

All of these examples show the name Prometheus being associated with knowledge and technology. If we examine the list carefully, we notice that these technologies are not just any technologies, but biology specific, dealing with life on a genetic (DNA) level. An angel named Prometheus may or may not exist, but people all around the world believed something gave them advanced technology at some point in our past. There are three other stories that should also catch our attention when it comes to advanced ancient technology.

Chapter 8: The Technology of Angels

- The Tower of Babel
- The Lost City of Atlantis
- Mahabharata

"And Azâzêl taught men to make swords, and knives, and shields, and breastplates, and made known to them the metals of the earth and the art of working them, and bracelets, and ornaments, and the use of antimony, and the beautifying of the eyelids, and all kinds of costly stones, and all colouring tinctures. And there arose much godlessness, and they committed fornication, and they were led astray, and became corrupt in all their ways. Semjâzâ taught enchantments, and root-cuttings, Armârôs the resolving of enchantments, Barâqîjâl, taught astrology, Kôkabêl the constellations, Ezêqêêl the knowledge of the clouds, Araqiêl the signs of the earth, Shamsiêl the signs of the sun, and Sariêl the course of the moon." – Enoch 8:1-3

The story of Atlantis speaks of a very advanced race of people that built a super weapon. Depending on which version of the story we read, it was destroyed by this weapon or some other kind of disaster. The people that escaped the city then migrated to different parts of the world. An interesting set of hieroglyphics found in Egypt depicts what seem to be airplanes and helicopters. How did the Egyptians develop knowledge of flying machines over 3,000 years ago?

Finally we get to the Mahabharata, which is dated around 6,500 B.C. It is probably the strangest story of all the ancient stories about technology because of its mention of nuclear weapons. Google "ancient nuclear war" and this excerpt from the story will pop up:

"A single projectile charged with all the power of the Universe. An incandescent column of smoke and flame As bright as the thousand suns Rose in all its splendor... a perpendicular explosion with its billowing smoke clouds... the cloud of smoke rising after its first explosion formed into expanding round circles like the opening of giant parasols... it was an unknown weapon, An iron thunderbolt, A gigantic messenger of death, Which reduced to ashes The entire race of the Vrishnis and the Andhakas. ...The corpses were so burned As to be unrecognizable. The hair and nails fell out; Pottery broke without apparent cause, and the birds turned white. After a few hours All foodstuffs were infected... ...to escape from this fire the soldiers threw themselves in streams to wash themselves and their equipment."[9]

The Breakdown

History is full of examples of technology that came from the heavens. Could these stories have been influenced by fallen angels interacting with mankind? The evidence points to this being exactly what happened. As humans we like to believe that we are the most advanced civilization in history, but if we look at the ancient myths and legends, there were other cultures that claim to witness the same technologies that we posses currently. When we look around at the technology available to us today, we need to be aware that its source may not be entirely of human origin.

Chapter in Review

- Do angels have access to technology?
- What are the merkabah?
- Are fallen angels trying to deceive people into believing in ancient aliens?
- Does human sacrifice have any connection to supernatural events?
- Is it possible that angels have influenced advances in human technology?

Critical Thinking

- What technology have angels given to mankind?
- Are modern day UFO sightings really merkabah?
- Will fallen angels return to earth to deceive mankind?
- Do people still participate in human sacrifice?

---

[9] Mahabharata

Chapter 8: The Technology of Angels

The Plan of Salvation

The plan of salvation is not difficult or complicated at all. In fact it can be summed up in one single verse. All you need to do in order to be saved is the following:

> That if thou shalt confess with thy mouth the Lord Jesus, and shalt believe in thine heart that God hath raised him from the dead, thou shalt be saved." – Romans 10:9

Key Scriptures For Review

- 2 Kings 2
- 2 Kings 17
- Psalms 106
- Isaiah 66
- Ezekiel 1
- Daniel 10
- Matthew 24
- 1 Corinthians 13
- Revelation 14

Submit Your Questions

If you have more questions about spiritual warfare, angels, demons, the supernatural, or the Bible in general, you are welcome to submit your questions to me personally. Answers to your questions will be posted as an article on the website for everyone to see.

www.MinisterFortson.com

Chapter 9: Supernatural Deception

> "All warfare is based on deception. Hence, when able to attack, we must seem unable; when using our forces, we must seem inactive; when we are near, we must make the enemy believe we are far away; when far away, we must make him believe we are near." — Sun Tzu: The Art of War

In Matthew 24:4, Jesus told the disciples, "take heed that no *thing* deceives you." The English translation says "no man" but the actual Greek text says "no thing". It is my personal belief that every word in the original language was chosen with a purpose in mind. Why would Jesus say thing (*tis*) instead of man (*anthropos*)? Possibly because mankind is not the only deceptive entity that we need to be aware of. As Christians, we also have to be aware of the deception of fallen angels and demons, as well as mankind. In this chapter we will explore several deceptive, but slightly convincing teachings from different cultures. The best deceptions are mixed with enough truth, so as not to raise suspicions.

Wrapped in Scripture

One of the most common ways that deceptive teachings enter into the church is by combining them with scripture. The Raeliens, for example, mostly quote sections of the Bible that agree with their doctrine, and if it does not, they will twist and misquote verses so that they do fit. On the surface it sounds Biblical until you realize that they are teaching that God, Satan, and Jesus are all extraterrestrials. They will also resort to using the Strong's Concordance to find the Hebrew words, but use a Zechariah Sitchin based definition to spread the message that the word means something other than the correct meaning. For those that are unfamiliar with some of these words, it sounds legitimate and they ultimately become indoctrinated with something that they believe is supported by the Bible, but in reality is not.

The Story of Creation

The creation story is one story that is found all over the world. Much like many other similar stories, the names and details are different, but the overall plot is the same:

- There is a Creator.
- He creates less powerful godlike beings.
- They form a rebellion.
- There is a war for control of heaven.
- One group is cast to earth.
- Humans are created.
- The lesser godlike beings torment mankind.
- Demigods are born on earth.
- The earth is wiped out with a flood.

Most religions and beliefs seem to follow that basic storyline. There are two possibilities here.

- These stories are based on real events.
- These stories are all made up.

Opinion: The chances of people from all over the world creating the exact same story line, containing very similar events, all while having different social, economic, and religious experiences is not likely.

The goal of the enemy is to steal, kill, and destroy (John 10:10). He is also smart enough not to deny the truth. His tactic seems to be to leave the core truth intact, but to redirect who that truth is applied to and how it is applied. One very interesting version of events comes from the Greek poet Hesiod. His theory on The Five Ages of Mankind closely matches many elements of the Bible, but with a twist of focus on who is responsible for what.

The Creation Deception

Hesiod was a Greek historian that believed that there was a previous race of human like beings, created before the current

Chapter 9: Supernatural Deception

race of man that lived in paradise and never aged. He believed that they died when they were very old, but at death they were transformed into spirits that now interact with and watch over mankind. He referred to them as the Golden Race. Interestingly, there is a very controversial subject in the Bible that may indeed support Hesiod's belief. We refer to this belief as The Gap Theory.

> "It is said that *people lived among the gods, and freely mingled with them*. Peace and harmony prevailed during this age. Humans did not have to work to feed themselves, for the earth provided food in abundance. They lived to a very old age but with a youthful appearance and eventually died peacefully. Their spirits live on as guardians." Plato in Cratylus

Many Christians believed that angels are manlike beings that guard or watch over mankind, and are commonly referred to as guardian angels. Part of the reason that Christians believe in guardian angels is because of the following verse which seems to imply that children have angels assigned to watch over them.

> "Take heed that ye despise not one of these little ones; for I say unto you, That in heaven their angels do always behold the face of my Father which is in heaven." - Matthew 18:10

Plato also mentions that these people lived among the gods, which deserves an explanation. In several cultures there is a single god that has multiple natures, similar to the Christian idea of the Trinity. Even the translators of the Bible found it difficult to determine whether the Serpent in the garden was referring to God or gods in the following statement.

> "For God doth know that in the day ye eat thereof, then your eyes shall be opened, and ye shall be as gods, knowing good and evil." - Genesis 3:5

In some modern churches the pastor will replace the word gods with God. The reason for this is because the Hebrew word is *"elohim"*, which is a plural word. However, when used with a singular verb it refers to a singular God. This can be seen in

Genesis 1:1 where it is translated as God, and in 1 Samuel 28:13 where the same word is translated as gods. It is entirely possible, but not provable that the Greeks had some understanding of the Trinity, but lacked the proper context to interpret who God really is. Again, this is just speculation, but a very interesting insight into the possible timeframe when angels existed before mankind.

Hesiod's Five Ages of Mankind also provides even more valuable insights into another commonly held set of beliefs that seem to be worldwide. This belief is that humanity has gone through different cycles or ages. In Christianity, this is commonly referred to as a "dispensation". There are three different Christian dispensation models that break down human history into sections of time in which God deals with humanity.

Model #1 (8 Dispensations)

1. Innocence (Genesis 1-3)
2. Conscience (Genesis 3-8)
3. Civil Government (Genesis 9-11)
4. Patriarchal (Genesis 12-19)
5. Mosaic (Exodus 20 until birth of the Church)
6. Grace (Church until the Rapture)
7. Millennium (Revelation 20:4-6)
8. Final (Revelation 20-22)

Model #2 (4 Dispensations)

1. Patriarchal (Genesis 1- Exodus 19)
2. Mosaic (Exodus 20 until birth of the Church
3. Ecclesial (Church until the Rapture)
4. Zionic (Revelation 20-22)

Model #3 (3 Dispensations)

1. Law (Genesis 1 until the birth of the Church)
2. Grace (Church until the Rapture)
3. Kingdom (Revelation 20-22)

As we can see, there are some Christians that divide the Biblical timeline by how God deals with mankind. On the other hand, Hesiod divides time based on the description of the type of people that exist.

> **Golden Age** – This is the time period which we discussed above. This race of men died and became guardians of the current creation of man. Plato in Cratylus (397 e) recounts the golden race of men who came first. He clarifies that Hesiod did not mean men literally made of gold, but good and noble. He describes these men as daemons upon the earth.

We are going to stop here for a moment, because something interesting begins to develop after Hesiod's first age. This Golden Age was made up of men that were not physically part of the following ages. In fact, all of the following four ages overlap, with the Gold Age being the only age that occurred before modern humans existed. On one hand, Hesiod describes this dead race as guardians and Plato describes these beings as *daemon*. The Greek word *daemon* means "knowledge" or "knowledgeable one." There is a reason that the word seems very similar to the word "demon", and that is because it is the word that is translated as devil/demon in our King James Bibles. Perhaps the most interesting thing about the entire theory is that both Hesiod and Plato associate this previous race of men with two different types of supernatural entities, similar to those found in the Bible. It is important to note that *daemon* were not always considered by the Greeks to be evil. For now, lets look at the last four ages of Hesiod.

> **Silver Age** - Men in the Silver age lived for one hundred years under the dominion of their mothers. They lived only a short time as grown adults, and spent that time in strife with one another. During this Age *men refused to worship the gods* and Zeus destroyed them for their impiety. After death, humans of this age became "blessed spirits" of the underworld.

There are several things worth mentioning about the silver age and its possible connection to the Bible. The first is that unlike the Bible, the men of this age only lived a short time. Short age and Zeus aside, it is the mention of refusing to "worship the gods" that is also of interest. If this period had to be connected to a Biblical time frame, it would be during the time of Adam. The reason that it may be connected to Adam's timeframe is because it was Seth's son that started to profane God's name and refused to worship Him.

> "The traditional Jewish interpretation of this verse, though, implies that it marked the beginning of idolatry, i.e. that men started dubbing "Lord" things that were mere creatures. This is because the previous generations, notably Adam, had already "begun calling upon the name of the Lord", which forces us to interpret *huchal* not as "began" but as the homonym "profaned". In this light, Enos suggests the notion of a humanity (Enoshut) thinking of itself as an absolute rather than in relation to God."[1]

In Hesiod's timeframe we find the first mention of the Underworld, which is where both Paradise and Hell were located. We find this same proximity in the Bible, in the parable of Lazarus and The Rich Man (Luke 16:26). Please keep in mind that this is all just interesting speculation that may or may not be right, but it is important to be as informed as possible when dealing with spiritual warfare. The other reason is that it actually establishes a very interesting spiritual pattern that goes hand in hand with the Bible. The next two ages actually seem to fit the pre-flood timeline.

Bronze Age - Men of the Bronze Age were hard. War was their purpose and passion. Not only arms and tools, but their very homes were forged of bronze. The men of this age were undone by their own violent ways and left no named spirits but dwell in the "dank house of Hades". It came to an end with the flood of Deucalion.

This period would be most similar to the time surrounding Noah's flood. In my previous book, <u>As The Days of Noah Were</u>, there is a list of the similarities of the over 500 flood stories from around the world. Notice that this period of Hesiod is marked with violence and ends with a flood, just as the Bible tells us.

> "And God said unto Noah, The end of all flesh is come before me; for the earth is filled with violence through them; and, behold, I will destroy them with the earth." – Genesis 6:13

---

[1] http://en.wikipedia.org/wiki/Enos_(Bible)

Chapter 9: Supernatural Deception

The Bronze Age of man and the following two ages are perhaps the closest fit to the Biblical narrative that we find in Greek literature. As we are about to see, there are two very strange references to unnatural activity taking place after the flood.

> **Heroic Age** - The Heroic Age is the one age that does not correspond with any metal. It is also the only age that improves upon the age it follows. In this period *men lived with noble demigods and heroes*. It was the heroes of this Age who fought at Thebes and Troy. This race of humans died and went to Elysium.

According to the Greeks, the demigods and heroes were half man and half god. According to legend, the gods lusted for human women and would go to great lengths to trick them into having sex and in some cases would simply rape the women that would not comply. According to the Bible, this took place before and after Noah's flood, but the Bible attributes these actions to the fallen angels.

> "And it came to pass, when men began to multiply on the face of the earth, and daughters were born unto them, That the sons of God saw the daughters of men that they were fair; and they took them wives of all which they chose. And the LORD said, My spirit shall not always strive with man, for that he also is flesh: yet his days shall be an hundred and twenty years. There were giants in the earth in those days; and also after that, when the sons of God came in unto the daughters of men, and they bare children to them, the same became mighty men which were of old, men of renown." - Genesis 6:1-4

This belief that supernatural beings that descended from the sky in order to have sex with human women is not new, in fact, it was accepted as part of the history of many cultures, including the following:

- Egypt
- Babylon
- Rome
- China
- India

All of these cultures have stories of this event occurring both before and after the great flood in Noah's time. In some of these stories, the gods frequented the cities and even ruled the people in some cases, such as the first two Egyptian Dynasties, and the Anunnaki in Babylon. This brings us to the final age of Hesiod, which echoes much of New Testament commentary on the last days.

> **Iron Age** - Hesiod finds himself in the Iron Age. During this age humans live an existence of toil and misery. Children dishonor their parents, brother fights with brother and the social contract between guest and host (xenia) is forgotten. During this age might makes right, and bad men use lies to be thought good. At the height of this age, humans no longer feel shame or indignation at wrongdoing; babies will be born with gray hair and *the gods will have completely forsaken humanity*: "there will be no help against evil."

If you are familiar with the Olivet Discourse then Hesiod's words should sound familiar. Much of what Jesus told his disciples are contained in this short description, along with verse found elsewhere in the New Testament. Here is a bulleted list of the attributes of this period according to Hesiod, along with the corresponding verses from the Bible.

- Children dishonor parents (Mark 13:12)
- Brother against brother (Mark 13:12)
- Lies and deception (Matthew 24:4)
- No remorse for wrongdoing. (Matthew 24:12)
- The gods forsake humanity. (2 Peter 3:4)

The last point, "the gods forsake humanity", is one of the points Hesiod makes that deserves a more in depth look. Peter makes this exact same point as one of the signs of the end of the age. People feel like Christ has abandoned them and begin to question why He has not yet returned.

Hesiod was by no means a Christian and he certainly did not just make all this stuff up off the top of his head. He had to be getting his spiritual insights from some source. Before Hesiod ever pulled out his quill to write, the book of Daniel gives almost the exact same description of five world empires which use the same metals that Hesiod used in his description of the

Chapter 9: Supernatural Deception

five ages. In Daniel 2 we find details of the last five world empires summarized as follows:

- Head: Gold
- Chest and Arms: Silver
- Belly: Brass
- Legs: Iron
- Feet: Iron and Clay

Both Hesiod and Daniel 2 have something interesting in common. Hesiod is considered a pagan, non Jewish historian, and the vision in Daniel 2 was received by the pagan, non Jewish king Nebuchadnezzar. While we cannot say for sure that Hesiod was influenced by Daniel or received a vision from God, it would not be out of the realm of possibility for that to be exactly the situation when he wrote about the five ages of man from his pagan perspective.

The Intelligent Design Deception

The Intelligent Design (ID) movement is becoming somewhat popular among Christians. The movement is best known for taking a scientific approach to the origin of the universe and everything in it. They believe that Intelligent Design should be taught in school along with Evolution. Because of the above mentioned movement, many people, including non-Christians, believe it is a completely Christian cause. What many people do not know is that ID is not 100% focused on teaching God or the Bible. The entire movement is about acknowledging a creator. There are many groups that support ID and acknowledge a creator, but they are by no means Christians nor are they referring to the God of the Bible when they make the claim that there is a creator.

- Raeliens
- Ancient Astronaut Theorists
- Wiccans
- Pagans

Once again, we see an example of the core truth of creation being redirected to aliens, gods, and goddesses. Getting ID put into schools may cause more harm than good, especially with the direction the world is going with the alien pop culture. Paul warns us about a twisting of the truth involving creation in the book of Romans:

> "Because that, when they knew God, they glorified him not as God, neither were thankful; but became vain in their imaginations, and their foolish heart was darkened. Professing themselves to be wise, they became fools, And changed the glory of the uncorruptible God into an image made like to corruptible man, and to birds, and fourfooted beasts, and creeping things." - Romans 1:21-23

Opinion: This verse is a direct reference to the lie of evolution, which clearly assigns the origin of mankind to gradual change of animals that existed prior to human beings.

The shift toward the belief in alien creators encompasses all belief systems without causing an offense to the majority of people. There are two major beliefs about how life came to exist on this planet.

- Creation
- Evolution

The alien creator hypothesis satisfies those that see the clear evidence of a creator, but it also espouses evolution as their means of creating life. Humanity is providing the perfect opportunity for the fallen angels to usurp the worldwide worship of God by presenting themselves as our alien creators. There is no deception more powerful than one that can be experienced by all of the human senses.

> "And for this cause God shall send them strong delusion, that they should believe a lie: That they all might be damned who believed not the truth, but had pleasure in unrighteousness." - 2 Thessalonians 2:11-12

There is a lot of speculation as to what this delusion will be, but there are many, including myself, that think this delusion will somehow involve an "alien" presence. If it is indeed spiritual in nature, the doorway and the invitation has been provided by millions of people on the planet that are waiting and welcoming E.T. as the saviors of humanity. For a more in depth study on the link between extraterrestrials and fallen angels, refer to my book, As The Days of Noah Were.

Angelic and Demonic Deception

Believe it or not, there is actually a connection between this deception and the ID deception. Those that wish to provide a more naturalistic explanation to Biblical events are attributing the appearance of angels in the Bible to extraterrestrials. They have redefined angels as being misinterpretations of beings from another planet. The History Channel is vigorously pushing this view through their TV series, Ancient Aliens, and many people are falling into this belief system.

As we dig further into this belief system we find what are called "walk-ins". This is when an alien entity is channeled and it possesses the human body, much like the demons in the Bible. This belief explains away evil demonic spirits and replaces them with highly evolved extraterrestrials exhibiting abilities that we are not yet capable of. The question now becomes, "why is our belief system changing to include an alien reality?"

Giving Heed To Seducing Spirits

It appears that we are entering a portion of history that is going to catch many people off guard, including Christians that do not take the Bible literally or seriously. As stated many times throughout this book, lack of research and insisting to hold on to antiquated tradition is a deadly flaw in the modern church, and will inevitably bring about the fulfillment of Hosea 4:6 in regards to the Church. The following verse is one of the most straight forward verses in the Bible concerning spirits and the end time scenario. It is very straight forward and disturbing in the Greek.

> "Now the Spirit speaketh expressly, that in the latter times some shall depart from the faith, giving heed to seducing spirits, and doctrines of devils;" – 1 Timothy 4:1

The problem is that many Christians downplay this verse as if it is only referring to doctrines that they perceive to be demonic. This is true in a sense, but notice that there is a differentiation made between the doctrine and the spirits themselves. The word "and" indicates that there will be multiple deceptions occurring and not just demonic doctrine. When we look at the Greek word for "seducing", this verse begins to take on an entirely different perspective. First let's look at the English word "seducing".

Seducing: to lead astray, as from duty, rectitude, or the like; corrupt.

The intent of these spirits is to lead people astray, but the current belief system of evolution is not as effective as many people think it is. Many people are starting to see the flaws in the theory and it is beginning to be called into question. As mentioned above, something stronger and more deceptive is needed.

Giving Heed: *prosecho* (Greek) meaning to give full attention or devotion to.

This will not just be a simple listening to these seducing spirits, but a full devotion to these spirits by people that once considered themselves to be Christians, which is what is implied by "depart from the faith". Again, this deception will have to be so strong that even Christians will step away from their faith to follow these spirits.

Seducing: *planos* (Greek) meaing to wander, mislead, deceive, or impersonate (imposter).

Paul's choice to use the word *planos* in this verse is interesting because of its root word. The Greek root for *planos* is *planao*, which is also the root of another word used by Jude in reference to the fallen angels.

Chapter 9: Supernatural Deception

> "Raging waves of the sea, foaming out their own shame; wandering stars, to whom is reserved the blackness of darkness forever." – Jude 1:13

Jude starts off by stating that he is going to put us in remembrance of something even though it was once known. From there he begins talking about the "angels that sinned", and comparing them to Sodom, Gomorrah, and Noah's flood. By the time we get to verse 13, he refers to them as "wandering stars". In Job 38 and Revelation 1, the angels are referred to as stars. The word "wandering" is the Greek word *planetes*, which is where we get the English word "planet". The root word of *planetes* is *planao*, just like the word *planos*, which Paul used. If we look at the origin of the English word planet, we can clearly make the connection here.

Planet: Origin: 1250-1300; Middle English planete (< Old French planète) < Late Latin planēta, planētēs (found only in plural planētae) < Greek (astéres) planḗtai literally, wandering (stars).[2]

Notice that the word means "wandering stars". Why would both Paul and Jude choose words that associate the fallen angels with planets? Why would Job and Jesus make reference to the angels as stars? Job made the reference in the Old Testament and Jude starts by saying that he wants to put us in remembrance of past events. Both Paul and Jesus are referring to prophetic future events involving angels.

Opinion: I believe the Bible was inspired by the Holy Spirit and as a result, I believe every word was chosen with a specific purpose in mind. While it is possible that this is a coincidence, all evidence points to it being much more than a mere coincidence in language.

The warning seems to be that these deceptive spirits in the last days will have some sort of connection to stars or planets. People are almost guaranteed to perceive these as highly evolved and advanced extraterrestrial beings, but the Bible is clear that these will be fallen angels out to deceive mankind.

---

[2] http://dictionary.reference.com/browse/planet

The Breakdown

As we have seen throughout this entire chapter, all of Christian theology is being attacked, redefined, and replaced with a naturalistic explanation of events. Many Christians have taken the ostrich approach by burying their head in the sand and completely ignoring the subject entirely. There are even some that go out of their way to criticize other Christians for warning people about this deception that is taking over society. The sad fact is that these Christians that are ignoring the issue are part of the reason people are turning to secular explanations. Many mainstream churches rely on tradition instead of investigating what the Bible says about matters such as the ones discussed above.

If we continue to completely ignore these changing beliefs and allow them to go on unopposed, we will be contributing to the great "falling away" that the Bible refers to in 2 Thessalonians 2:3 and 1 Timothy 4:1. This final deception is Satan's last attempt to save himself from the Lake of Fire and take as many souls with him in the process. People can label it as science fiction or fringe Christianity, but labels do not define what is truth, and the truth is that we are all being set up for the biggest deception to ever face mankind.

Chapter in Review

- Who are the Raeliens?
- What does mythology have in common with the Biblical account of creation?
- Is the Intelligent Design movement potentially dangerous to the Christian faith?

Critical Thinking

Chapter 9: Supernatural Deception

- Is deception more effective when it is wrapped in scripture?
- Should the Church completely ignore deceptive doctrines?
- Should the Church uphold tradition when it is in clear conflict with what the Bible teaches?

Key Scriptures For Review

- Genesis 3
- Genesis 6
- Matthew 18:10
- Romans 1
- 2 Thessalonians 2
- 1 Timothy 4
- Jude 1

The Plan of Salvation

The plan of salvation is not difficult or complicated at all. In fact it can be summed up in one single verse. All you need to do in order to be saved is the following:

> That if thou shalt confess with thy mouth the Lord Jesus, and shalt believe in thine heart that God hath raised him from the dead, thou shalt be saved." – Romans 10:9

Submit Your Questions

If you have more questions about spiritual warfare, angels, demons, the supernatural, or the Bible in general, you are welcome to submit your questions to me personally. Answers to your questions will be posted as an article on the website for everyone to see.

www.MinisterFortson.com

Chapter 10: The Destiny of Creation

"Sow a thought, and you reap an act; Sow an act, and you reap a habit; Sow a habit, and you reap a character; Sow a character, and you reap a destiny" – Charles Reade

After it is all said and done, all of creation has a destiny and everyone, including the angels will face judgment. In this chapter we are going to look at the destiny of humans, angels, demons, heaven, hell, and earth.

The Destiny of Humans

There are many beliefs in regards to the ultimate destiny of human beings. Some of these beliefs are popular, but non-Biblical. Even some of the non-Biblical beliefs are being taught in churches as Biblical doctrine. Some of the beliefs currently being taught in churches are the following:

Annihilationism – This is the belief that sinners are completely destroyed instead of suffering forever in the Lake of Fire.

Limbo/Purgatory – The belief states that there is a place of purification and temporary punishment other than heaven and hell. Some believe that the living can pray for the souls in Purgatory and get the souls promoted to heaven.

Reincarnation/Earth Ages – This is the belief that human beings existed in a previous earth age as spiritual beings and were then born into flesh bodies during this earth age. According to this theory, our actions in the previous earth age determine our destiny in this earth age. This is a mixture of Eastern Philosophy and Christianity.

Everyone Goes To Heaven – This is the belief reflected at most funerals and politically correct churches. It is the idea that nobody will spend eternity in hell, and those that do go to hell will only be there on a temporary basis.

None of the above beliefs have any Biblical backing at all, and they all seek to avoid the problem of eternal punishment in hell. The Bible is 100% clear as to the need of accepting Christ or face eternity in hell. In fact, this is one of the reasons that God has been holding back His judgment for as long as He has.

> "The Lord is not slack concerning his promise, as some men count slackness; but is longsuffering to us-ward, not willing that any should perish, but that all should come to repentance." - 2 Peter 3:9

All men that have ever lived or ever will live have two possible destinies. They will either spend eternity in the Lake of Fire or eternity in heaven. It is totally up to us as individuals where we will spend eternity.

The Ultimate Dice Roll

In church we are usually taught that Judgment will be 100% based on whether or not we know Christ as our personal Lord and Savior. It sounds like it makes perfect sense in the context of the Biblical teaching on salvation, until we dig a little deeper. Almost all pagan cultures teach that men will be judged based on their good deeds, and not whether or not they accept Christ. Further research reveals that the unsaved will indeed be judged based on their good and bad deeds.

> "And I saw the dead, small and great, stand before God; and the books were opened: and another book was opened, which is the book of life: **and the dead were judged out of those things which were written in the books, according to their works.**" - Revelation 20:12

The above verse is talking about the 2nd Resurrection and the 2nd judgment, which occurs after the 1,000 year reign of Christ. There are several things we should pay attentions to, and the mention of multiple books is one of them. There are multiple books opened in addition to the Book of Life by which men are judged.

Opinion: The other books are used to weigh the good vs. the bad that a person has done over the course of their life. The Book of Life is then referred to in order to see if the person's name is listed.

Chapter 10: The Destiny of Creation

Most pagan cultures reflect the idea of a supernatural record keeper that "keeps the books" for the very purpose of judgment, Egypt being the most well known among those cultures that do. Is there Biblical evidence of a record keeper that records every event and word in our life?

> "But I say unto you, That every idle word that men shall speak, they shall give account thereof in the day of judgment." - Matthew 12:36

Jesus seems to be indicating that very detailed records are being kept for the purpose of Judgment Day. Is this the information that appears in those other books that are opened? It is very likely, but there is no way to know until it happens.

Opinion: God is just and fair, and in order to have a 100% fair trial, all of the evidence needs to be weighed. We are all guilty of sin, but very few people would call themselves a bad person. In the end, it will be the sins of the unsaved individual which will be used against them in the court of spiritual law.

Thankfully God has offered us unconditional immunity through the sacrifice of Christ. All we have to do is believe that He is who the Bible says He is, confess it with our mouth, and accept Him as our Savior. For those that do not, they will indeed receive the most thorough and fair trial to ever happen in history. Will any of them get into heaven? We have no idea how the judgment process works for those that were born before the Law (without The Law there is no sin) and Christ; so we cannot say for sure what the outcome will be for them. One thing is for sure, we do not want to be the holder of those dice.

The Destiny of Hell

For many people, hell is the ultimate place of torment for souls of the damned. While it may be true that hell is a place of torment, it is not the final resting place of unsaved souls. Even hell has a final destination:

> "And death and hell were cast into the lake of fire. This is the second death." - Revelation 20:14

Those people that have been sent to hell all throughout history will indeed ultimately end up in the Lake of Fire. Once again, it is not because God has sent them there, but because they have made the conscious decision to ignore God's road map to heaven.

The Destiny of Heaven and Earth

When God destroyed the earth in Noah's time, He made a covenant between Himself and the rest of creation. This covenant was signified by the creation of the rainbow. It forever remains a sign after the rain that God will never again destroy every living thing on earth or curse the ground.

> "And the LORD smelled a sweet savour; and the LORD said in his heart, I will not again curse the ground any more for man's sake; for the imagination of man's heart is evil from his youth; neither will I again smite any more everything living, as I have done. While the earth remaineth, seedtime and harvest, and cold and heat, and summer and winter, and day and night shall not cease." - Genesis 8:21-22

While God does promise never to destroy all living things on earth, there will be a few major changes after the return of Christ. According to the Bible, there will be a new heaven and a new earth created. We find references to this in four places:

- Isaiah 65:17
- Isaiah 66:22
- 2 Peter 3:13
- Revelation 21:1

This belief in a new heaven and new earth being created is also reflected in Norse mythology as well. Many Christians view this as a strictly New Testament concept, but strangely enough, the majority of the details concerning this transformation are

Chapter 10: The Destiny of Creation

found in the Old Testament book of Isaiah. According to the Bible, the following changes will take place:

- The past will be forgotten (Isaiah 65:17)
- There will be rejoicing in Jerusalem (Isaiah 65:18)
- No more crying (Isaiah 65:19)
- People will live at least 100 years (Isaiah 65:20)
- People will build houses (Isaiah 65:21)
- People will plant vineyards (Isaiah 65:21)
- People will eat (Isaiah 65:21)
- The elect will live as long as the trees (Isaiah 65:22)
- The elect will enjoy the work of their hands (Isaiah 65:22)
- Prayers will be answered before they are finished (Isaiah 65:24)
- The wolf and lamb will eat together (Isaiah 65:25)
- The lion will eat straw/hay (Isaiah 65:25)
- The serpent will eat dust (Isaiah 65:25)
- No more sea (Revelation 21:1)

Contrary to popular belief, the earth is never completely destroyed, but it does go through some major changes.

The Destiny of Angels

According to the Bible, the destiny of angels is to be judged at the end of the age by human beings (1 Corinthians 6:3). The Bible does not tell us if this will include all angels or just the angels that rebelled with Satan. Those angels that chose to rebel with Satan will eventually spend eternity in the Lake of Fire.

> "Then shall he say also unto them on the left hand, Depart from me, ye cursed, into everlasting fire, prepared for the devil and his angels:" - Matthew 25:41

While there are some fallen angels still free to roam the earth and cause destruction, some angels have already been locked up, pending a later judgment.

The Destiny of Demons

In the Bible we only see demons tormenting mankind, wreaking havoc, and causing destruction. Whether in the flesh as hybrids or as spiritual beings, there is no indication in scripture of a single demon that is interested in salvation. In the New Testament we get a hint that demons already know their final destination is pending and it will not be good.

> "And, behold, they cried out, saying, What have we to do with thee, Jesus, thou Son of God? art thou come hither to torment us before the time?" - Matthew 8:29

Based on the above verse, it seems to be Jesus that will hand out their final punishment, but the Bible is not clear as to when the judgment of demons will take place or how they will be judged. There are many researchers that believe the demons will be locked in Tartarus (Outer Darkness). While there are disagreements as to whether demons will ultimately end up in the Abyss or The Lake of Fire, the Bible is clear that the final destination of demons will be a place of torment.

The Breakdown

Everything and everyone has a final destination. People will end up spending eternity with Christ or in everlasting fire (Matthew 25:41), angels will either be let off the hook or cast into The Lake of Fire, and all demons will face a place of torment. All of God's creation has been given free will, and as a result, we may choose to use it to serve God or to defy Him. Ultimately it is our own decisions that will determine where we spend eternity.

> "And if it seem evil unto you to serve the LORD, choose you this day whom ye will serve; whether the gods which your fathers served that were on the other side of the flood, or the gods of the Amorites, in whose land ye dwell: but as for me and my house, we will serve the LORD." - Joshua 24:15

Chapter in Review

- What is the destiny of humans?
- Will non believers be judged by their works?
- What is the destiny of hell?
- What is the destiny of heaven and earth?
- What is the destiny of angels?
- What is the destiny of demons?

Critical Thinking

- How do people avoid going to hell?
- Can works earn a person salvation?
- Can angels obtain salvation?
- Can demons obtain salvation?

The Plan of Salvation

The plan of salvation is not difficult or complicated at all. In fact it can be summed up in one single verse. All you need to do in order to be saved is the following:

> That if thou shalt confess with thy mouth the Lord Jesus, and shalt believe in thine heart that God hath raised him from the dead, thou shalt be saved." – Romans 10:9

Key Scriptures For Review

- Genesis 8
- Joshua 24
- Isaiah 65
- Matthew 8
- Matthew 12
- Matthew 25
- 2 Peter 3

- Revelation 20

Submit Your Questions

If you have more questions about spiritual warfare, angels, demons, the supernatural, or the Bible in general, you are welcome to submit your questions to me personally. Answers to your questions will be posted as an article on the website for everyone to see.

www.MinisterFortson.com

Bonus Material and Resources

About The Author

Minister Dante Fortson was born November 15, 1982 in Las Vegas, NV, to Pastor Perryetta Lacy. As a child, growing up in his grandparents' house, Minister Dante Fortson had many experiences that have helped shape his belief in God and the supernatural. As a result of a dream one night and hearing his name being called in the house the following morning, he was saved and baptized at a very young age.

In elementary school he would read about vampires, ghosts, and other supernatural phenomena every chance he had. As he neared the 8th grade, Minister Fortson developed a sudden interest in UFOs, aliens, and the occult. One night, after a seemingly failed attempt to channel what he believed to be extraterrestrials, a life changing demonic experience left him with a lasting fear of the dark and led him to start studying the Bible more intensely for an explanation of the events. It has been a little over a decade since Minister Fortson became a student of Bible prophecy. Now, considered by many to be an expert in demonology, angelology, and the supernatural, he freely shares his knowledge and experience with anyone seeking advice in spiritual matters.

His goal is to provide a place where people can turn to and get solid Biblical answers about their supernatural experiences without the fear of ridicule that is often times present in mainstream churches. Minister Fortson believes that having a strong Biblical foundation is the key to understanding what people label as supernatural events. It is his belief that the Bible is of supernatural origin and contains truthful explanations of supernatural events that have occurred throughout history.

If you have a question in regards to the supernatural, you can contact Minister Fortson by visiting his website and sending him an email.

www.MinisterFortson.com

As The Days of Noah Were
The Sons of God and The Coming Apocalypse

What does the Bible really say about the last days on earth? Who were the sons of God? What were the strange beings known as the Nephilim? Did God really hide everything we need to know about the last days in the book of Genesis? Step by step we will journey through the days of Noah and piece together our coming future. We will explore stories from Sumer, Greece, and various other cultures to fill in the missing pieces to one of the biggest mysteries on our planet. Who were the sons of God and will they return?

"I recommend reading: 'As The Days of Noah Were', by Minister Dante Fortson. 'As The Days' is a well researched text, wonderfully fascinating. I've read a number of books on supernatural phenomenon - how such phenomenon manifests within our more understood physical reality - this book is among the best." - C. Heidt

"One thing I appreciate about this book (and Dante's ministry in general) is how he challenges believers to read the Scripture for themselves to verify what they're being taught and not just believe what they are taught because they're told it's true, when the teaching is nothing more than the traditions of men." - L. Holmes

"This book is amazing in its premise and conclusions. Very well researched and documented by the author. Literally, my view of the world and the Bible changed due to this book." - Stacey Harper

"After hundreds of hours of podcast listening to Dante and many other well educated hard working researchers, I found his book to be very well organized, full of vital information, and easy to read and understand. I learned a great deal more than I had previously digested from all the various podcasts and books which I'd poured through after my introduction to this "alternative" thinking which I know was brought to me by the Holy Spirit of God." - Christopher Moffitt

Scenario X: Seven Steps To Great Tribulation

The main part of prophecy that I've had trouble putting together is exactly how or why the world would come together under one leader. This scenario is based on a 3.5 year timeline (the first half of the Tribulation).

Step One

- Global disasters ravage the Earth, causing chaos and destruction.
- Animals and people die in mass.
- These set the stage for a possible 2012 disclosure.

Step Two

- A person of importance publicly declares, "if anybody is out there we could sure use their help" (Paraphrase).
- The above statement has already been purposely planned in advance.

Step Three

- The "alien saviors" arrive just in time to save us.
- People embrace them with open arms and assume they are benevolent.

Step Four

- They claim to be the God of the Bible, Allah, the angels, and various other deities from around the world. I
- In addition they claim to be behind the resurrection of Christ.
- They claim that with a combination of technology and evolution, they created mankind on this planet. This would instantly unify science and religion, causing many to fall away or depart from the faith and give heed to seducing spirits and doctrines of literal demons.
- Many will lose the need to believe in a supernatural God in favor of the new natural gods that have just arrived.

Step Five

- We are introduced to various races of "aliens" in order to solidify the validity of evolution.
- All of these races of aliens are really fallen angels in a shapeshifted form.
- They claim that we need to evolve spiritually and become like "gods" if we want to survive as a race.
- In order to do so we need to erase the boundary lines that separate us and be joined as one. This would create the official world empire.
- We also need to erase religious boundaries and put all faiths under a single umbrella religion.
- Once that is accomplished, they then suggest a man to lead this world into a New Age. This man turns out to be the Antichrist.

Step Six

- Everyone linked to Abraham (Christians, Jews, Muslims) will be persecuted for holding back mankind's spiritual evolution to become gods.
- Heavy persecution of any faith in the God of the Old Testament begins.
- Someone kills the Antichrist, which in turn allows the "alien" visitors to show their power and resurrect him.

Step Seven

- After the resurrection the AC enters the Holy of Hollies and declares himself to be the savior of mankind.
- This causes another huge falling away because of the false miracle.
- He then forces everyone to take a mark (**666**) to show their loyalty to him.
- We officially enter the last 3.5 years (Great Tribulation) of this current age.

Disclaimer: I am simply reviewing my own research and the research of others, and attempting to organize it as a **POSSIBLE** scenario. This should not in any way be considered a prophecy or a revelation from God.

Made in the USA
Columbia, SC
30 November 2022